MW01519669

"*Scattering the Sheep*
course correction.
course, but intrins.
calling sin what God calls it. When the churches closed – at
all – during the pandemic, it was sin. It was rebellion against
the clear teaching of God's Word on the issue of local church
assembly. Further, it was idolatry. A fear of death and illness
that superseded the fear of God that only He deserves.
Unless there is sincere repentance involving confession, we
cannot expect there to be any significant difference the next
time that politicians 'request' that our churches close for
what they consider to be an emergency."

Jon Speed
Elder, By the Word Baptist Church

"*Scattering the Sheep* should be read by every pastor in America.
Chris pulls no punches concerning the failures of the church
during Covid. However, he hits hard not as an enemy, but as
a brother in Christ. His love for Christ and the Church is in
every rebuke. So, as you read it remember the words of
David, 'Let a righteous man strike me – it is a kindness; let
him rebuke me – it is oil for my head; let my head not refuse
it' (Psalm 141:5)."

Joe Jewart
Pastor, Calvary Baptist Church

"It is understood that humanity has a habit of replicating past
mistakes. In other words, 'history repeats itself.' Without
honest reflection on what occurred in 2020, the American
Church is destined to continue this pattern. Chris Hume's
analysis of the recent stain within the American Church is a
solid Scriptural examination regarding the matter. *Scattering*
the Sheep should be part of every Christian's library."

Dave Coyle
Missionary, Love & Justice Ministries

"Scattering the Sheep is a resounding, Scripture-rooted call to repentance for any American pastor or elder who reacted to unconstitutional orders by closing their church doors to in-person worship for even one Sunday."

Jessica Hockett, Ph.D.
Social Media Influencer

"Given the shameless cooperation displayed by many churchmen in 2020 – cooperation that rendered many churches every bit as 'non-essential' as the state said they were – it is clear that the church of Jesus Christ cannot afford any more bad ideas. Churchmen cancelled the gathering of God's people, mandated masks, and even denied access to the Lord's table based on a Christian's unwillingness to submit to man-made traditions and ecclesiastical propriety. Many churchmen of all stripes, supposed promoters of the 'separation of church and state,' found themselves walking lockstep with governors and health officials. We cannot afford another pathetic display. Thus, the importance of this book."

Joel Saint
Pastor, Independence Reformed Bible Church

SCATTERING THE SHEEP

SCATTERING THE SHEEP

A Jeremiad Concerning the Closing of the American Church in 2020

CHRIS HUME

MOUNTVILLE, PENNSYLVANIA

Published by The Lancaster Patriot
125 Oakridge Drive, Mountville, Pennsylvania 17554
717.370.7508 | www.thelancasterpatriot.com

Christopher Hume, *Scattering the Sheep: A Jeremiad Concerning the Closing of the American Church in 2020*

A man really believes not what he recites in his creed, but only the things he is willing to die for.

Richard Wurmbrand

Wounds cannot be healed until they are revealed, and sins cannot be forgiven until they are confessed.

Martin Luther

CONTENTS

ACKNOWLEDGMENTS

Thanks to Joel Saint for, among many other things in my life, indirectly giving me the idea for the title of this book. Thanks to Matt Trewhella for his example and his willingness to write the foreword to this book. Thanks to John Bingaman for providing feedback on the manuscript. Thanks to my lovely wife, Bess, for all her support and encouragement. And, finally, thanks and praise to the Lord Jesus, the Great Shepherd of the sheep, for being so kind to his church so as not to leave us with only pastors who scattered the sheep in 2020, but also with a handful who remained faithful.

FOREWORD

In March of 2020 a national emergency was declared by the President of the United States with the following words:

> Now, therefore, I, Donald J. Trump, President of the United States, by the authority vested in me by the Constitution and the laws of the United States of America, including sections 201 and 301 of the National Emergencies Act (50 U.S.C. 1601 et seq.) and consistent with section 1135 of the Social Security Act (SSA), as amended (42 U.S.C. 1320b-5), do hereby find and proclaim that the COVID-19 outbreak in the United States constitutes a national emergency, beginning March 1, 2020.

Shortly after that pronouncement, churches were declared "non-essential" by state governments across the nation and were either ordered or strongly advised to shut down. The compliance by churchmen[1] was blithe and near monolithic – approximately 95% of churches shuttered their doors.

---

[1] Christian leaders and pastors.

Looking back, one wonders how it was that the vast majority of churchmen and Christians could not see Covid for the fraud that it was. Mercy Seat Christian Church, our assembly in Wisconsin, was kicked out of our meeting place in March of 2020. The very next week our church began meeting in homes and we have never stopped gathering since. On March 29, 2020, I delivered a sermon entitled, "COVID-19 & Quarantine Laws."[2] In that message, I preached on Leviticus 13 and declared:

> You do not quarantine the whole of society, you quarantine the sick…Notice in God's law that the rights and freedoms of the entire population are not abridged just because there is disease…Please understand, disease is always around in any society. You cannot spend your life hiding from germs, viruses, and diseases.

And yet, most churchmen spent months and months kowtowing to government mandates and man-made edicts. Churchmen shut down their churches, appealing to a servile submission to the state or a nanny-like desire to prevent their people from making their own decisions about gathering.

How was it that they could not discern that government officials were using Covid as a tool for evil designs? How could they not see it was a molehill being made into a mountain? How could they not see it for the fraud and evil that it was? How could they not see the Covid response as pure evil when it

[2] Available at www.tinyurl.com/trewhellacovid

impugned God's created order by preventing men from working (deeming their jobs "non-essential")? How could they not see it for the fraud and evil that it was when the churches were labelled "non-essential," but the abortion deathcamps were deemed "essential" and remained open? How could they not see it for the fraud and evil that it was when God's law makes it clear that only the sick are to be quarantined – but the government officials were quarantining the whole of society? Why did it take months before some began to see it? And why do many *still* believe it?

Why were the churchmen putty in the hands of wicked men who employed them to further convince the people that the Covid response was not a lie, not a fraud, not a great evil? How could they not discern that evil was afoot?

The answer to these questions is – in part – because the most vaunted desire of your average American churchman is to be liked. He wants to be thought well of, and he loves the praises of men. In America, therefore, the average churchman wants to be a consensus-builder, not a servant leader whose fealty is first to the Lord and His law. The average American churchman also wants nothing to do with confrontation. And so, timid responses and weak knees befit him. But American churchmen must understand this: The Gospel itself is confrontational.

The message of the Gospel confronts the individual and his sin. Furthermore, the Gospel confronts the evils, idols, and tyrants of a nation. As such, Christianity has historically found itself in direct confrontation with the civil authorities. From the book of Acts forward, the Gospel has been in confrontation with individuals and pagan tyrants.

But American churchmen want to be liked, and they want nothing to do with confrontation. So, when Covid came along, their response was predictable. They joined in the chorus of hysteria, and they refused to confront lawless magistrates or expose the evil of their response to Covid. When the state ordered (or in other situations strongly advised) that the churchmen close their church doors – they closed their church doors. Many of their excuses for doing so will be examined in this book.

In the past, when pastors had backbones and men stood against evil, churchmen boldly barred the state from entering the church because they wanted to uphold the *authority* of the church and preserve righteousness. Ambrose stood down Emperor Theodosius and interposed at the door of the church. John Chrysostom, whose sermon can still be read today, preached about Eutropius while protecting him and refusing to allow state authorities to enter the church and take him.

But not today's churchmen – men incapable of blushing. When the state deemed the churches non-essential and ordered church doors closed in most states around the country, the churchmen affirmed what most already knew – they were *non-essential*. They closed their doors. They also had the audacity to claim to be obedient to God by quoting the Word of God and twisting Romans 13, among other passages.

These churchmen have long obeyed any and every edict of the state due to their bogus assertions about Romans 13, claiming that "we are to always obey the civil authorities." I had numerous ministers tell me that we are *dutybound* to obey the state and *cease* meeting based on Romans 13. So, I went to Romans 13 and simply pointed to the text found in verses 3 and 4:

> For Magistrates are not to be feared for good works, but for evil. Wilt thou then be without fear of the power? do well: so shalt thou have praise of the same. For he is the minister of God for thy wealth: but if thou do evil, fear: for he beareth not the sword for nought: for he is the minister of God to take vengeance on him that doeth evil.

And then I asked: "Does not Romans 13 make clear the function of civil government is to punish those who do *evil*? Is attending church evil?" I then asked: "Will you report us to the state authorities since we meet anyway?"

Churchmen *should* have kept their church doors open despite state orders, and despite the threats of a disease. As this book points out, it is not the churchmen's job to make health choices for Christians. But sadly, instead of interposing against the state, American churchmen conformed to the state.

Interposition is a historic Christian doctrine

practiced by the church and found in Scripture. One interposes when he stands in the gap between the oppressor and his intended victim. The magistrates are to be opposed if they make law or policy contrary to the Word of God, or if they exceed the limits of their authority. The church has a long history of standing in interposition against the state, and had the churches interposed in our day, the evil of the magistrates would have been seriously blunted. The churchmen, however, told us that good Christians will obey and go along because that is "loving" and "we don't want to hurt our witness."

The truth is, faithful Christians don't spread lies, and they don't aid and abet tyrant government officials by helping spread their lie. *This whole Covid matter was built on lies.*

The churchmen said you were not loving your neighbor if you kept gathering on the Lord's Day. The churchmen said you were not loving your neighbor if you did not wear the mask when they finally opened the church doors. Some even said you were hurting your witness if you did not wear the mask.

The opposite was actually the truth. If you wore the mask, and even more so if you required it of your parishioners, you were not showing love to others because you joined in a great lie. The ninth commandment comes to bear here – "Thou shalt not bear false witness." When you wore the mask, I submit that you were partaking in the lie, acting as if the fiction was fact. Exodus 23:1-2 (ESV) states:

You shall not spread a false report. You shall not join hands with a wicked man to be a malicious witness. You shall not fall in with the many to do evil, nor shall you bear witness in a lawsuit, siding with the many, so as to pervert justice.

Verse six of the "love chapter" (1 Corinthians 13) declares that love "rejoiceth not in iniquity, but rejoiceth in the truth." Churchmen failed to rejoice in the *truth*, and instead supported lies.

The fraud of the Covid response by the government was built on two mountains. A mountain of lies and a mountain of money. Many churchmen not only closed their churches and played the traitor, but they also played the whore. They took money from the state. They closed their doors, told parishioners to stay home, and took the money the government was handing out like candy.

In fact, over $12 billion in government money went to churches and religious organizations across America. When this money was made available, the Christian lawyers quickly moved in, and numerous Christian legal organizations taught the churchmen how to get their "free money" from the government. On August 3, 2020, NPR published the following:

> Religious organizations, having received as much as $10 billion in the first round of COVID-19 aid, hope to receive more funding under any new relief package. Churches of all denominations and other religious nonprofits were quick to take advantage of the Paycheck

Protection Program, which provided forgivable loans under the CARES Act in March…Mainline Protestant and evangelical churches also benefited. An analysis by Ministry Watch, an organization that provides guidance on charitable giving, reported this month that churches and other religious non-profits as a whole received between $6 and $10 billion in PPP funding…In a new report released this week, Ministry Watch identified more than 400 evangelical ministries and churches that each received at least $1 million in COVID-19 aid, with seven institutions receiving PPP loans of $5-10 million. Among those receiving multi-million dollar forgivable loans were some of the best known evangelical churches in the country, including the First Baptist Church of Dallas and Redeemer Presbyterian Church in New York City. Willow Creek Community Church in Barrington, Illinois, received $5-10 million in relief aid, as did the headquarters of the Evangelical Lutheran Church in America (ELCA).[3]

The churchmen lined up by the thousands to get the money. Paperwork and acknowledgements had to be made in agreement with the government to get your "free" money.[4] The American churchmen – by the

---

[3] "Religious Groups Received $6-10 Billion In COVID-19 Relief Funds, Hope For More," 3 August 2020. Retrieved from npr.org.

[4] Interestingly, John MacArthur claims the money just *showed up* at their church and they sent it back. However, in April of 2020, attorney Brian C. Brisco wrote, "The United States Small Business Administration ('SBA') has expressly indicated that faith-based organizations, including houses of worship, are eligible to *apply* for and receive PPP/EIDL loans" (emphasis added). Brisco went to answer the question of whether a church should *apply* for a PPP/EIDL loan, noting that the "decision can only be made by the decision makers in any particular church" (retrieved from

thousands – closed their doors and took the money. They lusted after the money like King Thorin lusted for the Arkenstone beneath the mountain of Erebor.

Starting near the end of July and early August of 2020 – right about the time the free money from the government was coming to an end – some of the churchmen began to reopen their doors. Amazingly enough, that is when John MacArthur and many of the churchmen – the pietistic pastors who had hitherto been compliant with state edicts – began to meet again.

During this whole debacle, as some churchmen began to reopen their churches, they adhered to all the social distancing and masking nonsense. The churchmen were paid by the state to teach Christian people to put on masks, sit six feet apart, put slimy stuff on their hands, and get the "vaccine." The churchmen were whores paid by the state to teach their people to obey tyrants – and some were not paid and did it *freely*. They joined in a lie and complied with an evil agenda. The social distancing and masking by governments was an extension of the statist hell America already was experiencing. It was a visible representation of how Americans have declared the *state* to be God, blithely rendering complete obedience to the state in all things.

Many said, "It's just a mask." Or, "We will only be shut down for a few weeks, it's not a big deal." But it was far more than that. The mandates were part and parcel of a great evil designed by wicked men and

www.canteyhanger.com).

statist governments.

We have forgotten that tyranny is built plank by plank. The Jews, for example, didn't just get called to the railway station one day to be stuffed into boxcars. Long before that, they were *first* told they could not sit on public park benches. And the Jews accommodated themselves to that. "It's just a park bench." (Just as many in our day said, "It's just a mask," or, "It's just a church service, we can still *be* the church in private.") Then, another law was passed, and the Jews accommodated themselves to that. And then another, and they accommodated themselves to that too. And then another and another. There are a thousand accommodations to evil before you get to the final solution.

We must guard the liberty we possess. Men fought, bled, and died to establish the freedom and liberty we possess – we have no right to glibly give it away.

The noted British statesman, William Pitt, once said: "Necessity is the plea for every infringement of human freedom. It is the argument of tyrants. It is the creed of slaves." And the tyrants of our day have learned that a virus is the perfect narrative to impose a tyranny on the citizenry, especially when craven churchmen will lead the way by embracing a babysitter mentality which turns their parishioners into toddlers unable to assess risk.

The tyranny of 2020 was evil, and it was a pernicious evil. Citizens were turned against one another. Government officials put up phone numbers to call and websites to visit to tell on your neighbors for not complying. Media outlets published countless articles and videos teaching citizens how to shame those not wearing the masks. We routinely saw posts and editorials stating that people who will not participate in the coming vaccination should have their children seized from them by the state.

When a climate of fear and authoritarianism grows, people will more and more ingratiate themselves to the ruling authorities by turning on their fellow citizens. Reporting them to Big Brother as Orwell described in *1984*, even making up stories and lies about them – just to make things better for themselves. History teaches these things time and again. These are matters of human nature.

James Madison warned in 1785 that any law which had the mere *potential* to curb liberty must be opposed:

> It is proper to take alarm at the first experiment on our liberties. We hold this prudent jealousy to be the first duty of Citizens, and one of the noblest characteristics of the late Revolution. The free men of America did not wait till usurped power had strengthened itself by exercise, and entangled the question in precedents. They saw all the consequences in the principle, and they avoided the consequences by denying the principle.

How is it that we must convince our fellow Christians that our civil government is prone to deal in falsehoods? How is that churchmen *still* believe the government officials were looking out for the best interests of the church of Jesus Christ? We should always have a healthy suspicion of government.

The most shocking trait of mankind – the thing that stuns me most and leaves me most dumbfounded about man – is his willingness to *conform*. That he will go along with most anything. Matters of injustice or immorality are of no consequence to him – he blithely conforms.

According to Webster, the definition of *conform* is "to obey or agree with something; to do what other people do; to behave and/or think in a way that is accepted by most people." Jesus understood this about the nature of man – his willingness to conform. It is revealed in His statement:

> Enter in at the strait gate: for it is the wide gate, and broad way that leadeth to destruction: and many there be which go in thereat. Because the gate is strait, and the way narrow that leadeth unto life, and few there be that find it. (Matthew 7:13-14)

When it comes to man's willingness to conform, Pink Floyd asked it this way:

> And did they get you to trade your heroes for ghosts? Hot ashes for trees? Hot air for a cool breeze? Cold comfort for change? And did you exchange a walk on part in the war for a lead role in a cage?

My mom put it this way, "If everyone else walked off the end of the pier, would you walk off too?" And

Thoreau said, "Any fool can make a rule, and any fool will mind it." That man is wont to conform has even been proven by experiments (the Asch and Milgram experiments and studies, for example). All studies left researchers shocked to see how people were willing to conform – even when they *knew* bad consequences would result; even when they *knew* what was being done was wrong or physically harmed others.

Now let us ask ourselves, *why* do people conform? Frankly, much of it has to do with being liked. This has to do with the fear of man. "What will others think of me?" Secondly, it has to do with authority. Those in authority influence those under them – for good or for bad. Both of these have an impact on how individuals conform.

The American people have been indifferent and compliant with every evil that has come down the pike. Americans have been indifferent and compliant with the slaughter of the preborn. They have been indifferent and compliant with homosex being decriminalized and sodomite "marriage" being legalized. They have been indifferent and compliant with clear affronts to the law and Word of God. And they were indifferent and compliant with the evil actions of their government regarding Covid. Excepting widespread repentance, these two traits – indifference and compliance – will be the undoing of America.

And the churchmen have aided and abetted it all. They have taught people that God is fine with this. They blindly submit and comply to anything the state decrees, and then with shrill voices they worry aloud about how all men tend towards rebellion and disobedience. They therefore demand complete obedience to the state – and to their coveted "pastoral authority" – lest this rebellion in man is unleashed.

I submit to you that the bigger danger in America today is not the *rebellion* of man *against* the state, but the *compliance* of man *to* the state – a compliance that was modelled by America's churchmen in 2020.

Churchmen talk all day about obeying the state. But what about when compliance becomes evil? What about when blithe obedience helps evil grow and strengthen? Churchmen talk all day about obeying the state as though the magistrates themselves cannot establish rebellion and lawlessness.

The churchmen herd the Christians into compliance with evil magistrates and then cover it all in sappy spiritual-sounding words. They take verses of Scripture out-of-context to buttress their aiding and abetting lawless government officials.

All of this reveals the need for true leadership in the church. Leadership tells people what they *need* to hear not what they *want* to hear. Leadership doesn't just go along to get along. Leadership doesn't blithely obey what the person above them tells them. Godly church leaders stand in the gap for their people. But American churchmen have proven themselves traitors and whores, and the pulpits have failed.

The Church in America lives in its hovel – smug in its indifference to public policy matters – and refuses to confront the idols, evils, and tyrants of our day, and is thus incapable of discerning evil when it is afoot. Inevitably, these churches, lacking discernment, are easily duped. They still think we are living in Mayberry R.F.D.

In summary, the churchmen fell for the lie – and will fall for the next one if they do not repent – because they want to fit in and be liked by the culture. The church has lost her prophetic role of forthtelling. And because confrontation has been labelled a vice, the American churchmen no longer call the institutions of our culture to repentance or reform when they do wrong. Instead, these weak men sit like lumps of putty, waiting to be shaped by the pagan rulers. As Herbert Schlossberg wrote in his magnum opus, *Idols for Destruction*:

> Civil religion eases tensions, where biblical religion creates them. Civil religion papers over the cracks of evil, and biblical religion strips away the covering, exposing the nasty places. Civil religion prescribes aspirin for cancer, and biblical religion insists on the knife.

Because the churchmen live in a pretend world of retreat and escape – of indifference to the evil in the land – they lack the ability to discern when something evil is taking place. And even if they do see it, they lack the courage to do what is necessary to oppose it.

Many dismissed the evil designs of the Covid response with the slogan "God is in control" or "God's got this." In other words, appeals were made to God's sovereignty to justify indifference and inaction. But the truth is God's sovereignty does not negate man's duty. God's sovereignty is not meant to be used as an excuse for our indifference. When we see the media and government speaking lies and enabling tyranny – we have a *duty* to speak and act against that. And when we see churchmen aiding and abetting the evil of the government officials – we have a duty to speak against that too.

Despite the discouraging response of churchmen, there is something to be encouraged about. The current weak form of Christianity is going to end in America and throughout Western Civilization. It cannot last. People often ask me, "How do we reform the church?" They ask this because they see the awful condition of American Christianity. And the answer is simple: by the judgment of God.

Understand, reader, that we have a form of Christianity in America that is incapable of *reforming itself* – but the Lord will reform His bride; He will purify her. When His people refuse to reform and purify themselves voluntarily, He uses judgment to bring that about. God's primary interest in judging America, His primary interest in unleashing the tyrants upon America, is to reform and purify His bride. Judgement begins in the house of the Lord.

The time has come for a tougher form of Christianity. A biblical, historical form of Christianity. One in which men can once again feel welcome. One in which men do not have to put their brains on a shelf and adorn themselves with effeminate trappings to be part of Christ's church. One in which the evils, idols, and tyrants will be taken to task by courageous churchmen. One in which shepherds stand firm, rather than caving before the pagan state, and scattering the sheep in the name of "safety" and "compliance."

And that is why this book is so important. What Chris Hume has given us here is a gem. This book provides a needed historical reminder of what took place in 2020, but even more importantly, it provides a needed call to *repentance*. May this work not only be a benefit to the men of our generation – but to the men of generations to come.

Pastor Matthew Trewhella
Richfield, Wisconsin
October 30, 2023

INTRODUCTION

COGNITIVE DISSONANCE

It was on August 16, 2023, that I knew this book had to be written.

I was preparing for an episode of *The Lancaster Patriot Podcast* and had posted a promotional graphic on social media for the upcoming show featuring authors of the 2020 book, *Coronavirus and the Leadership of the Christian Church: A Sacred Trust Broken*. Here is what I posted:

Has the church learned from Covid-19? Generally speaking, I am concerned she has not. Churches that shut down at the drop of a dime (like Grace Community Church in California) and then waited weeks and weeks to reopen (prompted not by the pastors but by the people) are now presenting themselves as models of faithfulness during the "plandemic." Does this whitewashing serve the church? I think not. These churches have still not addressed the fact that they should have never shut down at all; and if another "threat" arises, I expect they would do the same all over again. Another whitewashing is to say that all churches were shut down for weeks. This is simply not true. Those churches that did not shut down at all are the worthy examples, not a church that shut down for well over a month. Ernie Springer, who will be coming on *The Lancaster Patriot Podcast* this week, wrote: "[A]mongst the world of disillusioned people, the credibility of the Church has been diminished if not lost altogether in the minds of some who see church leaders' support of societal panic no different than secular culture whose trust is in themselves and in government control." He is correct. And David Engelsma, in endorsing Springer's book, noted that the book calls churches "to repentance (sorrow over past disobedience) and conversion (change of behavior)." That sorrow and change is lacking in most churches that shut down.

What happened next, however, shocked me.

A seminary-trained pastor, committed to the essential truths of the Christian faith, publicly responded to my post. What he wrote was almost unbelievable, especially given that I had pointed out the problem of whitewashing[1] in my initial post. Here is what he wrote:

> You might want to correct this, Chris. There was not a single Sunday where MacArthur was not behind the pulpit. He kept showing up and soon the people came back. They never shut down.

---

[1] Whitewashing is deliberately attempting to conceal unpleasant or incriminating facts about someone or something.

I had to do a doubletake. But there it was: "They never shut down."

My mind went almost immediately to George Orwell's *1984*. In that dystopian tale, the story's protagonist, Winston, works for the Records Department of the Ministry of Truth. His job is to rewrite the historical documents to match the Party's version of events. If past events don't serve the interests of the powers that be, they can simply be changed. My mind also went to our government's attempts to whitewash the past about Covid-19 – namely, Fauci backtracking on various claims he made about masks and mandates.

I don't know if the pastor who responded to my social media post had any ulterior motives or underlying schemes, like Orwell's Ministry of Truth or Anthony Fauci. But I was still very concerned. If this pastor, a level-headed evangelical leader, believes Grace Community Church "never shut down," then I am sure other people do as well. How could we so easily forget what happened just three years ago? And how does that bode for the future? If we are ignorant of what happened, how can we learn from it? Or, what if we *know* what happened, but simply don't want to accept it?

The fact of the matter is that Grace Community Church, led by John MacArthur, shut down *right away* when the government asked them to in 2020. I will address this more fully in Chapters 2 and 3, but for now, here is what MacArthur said when the government's shutdown orders were released: "The clear demand of Scripture is to be subject to the [civil government] …We conform, we are submissive to the government. *That was an easy call for us.*"[2]

COGNITIVE DISSONANCE

Cognitive dissonance is the perception of contradictory information in the mind and the subsequent mental anguish. Many evangelical and Reformed Christians are trying to hold two contradictory claims in their minds: (1) Pastors like John MacArthur are worthy examples of faithfulness, and (2) pastors like John MacArthur shut down their churches on the drop of a dime. The two claims don't jive.

On the aforementioned episode of *The Lancaster Patriot Podcast*, Joel Yeager, medical doctor and co-author of *Coronavirus and the Leadership of the Christian Church*, explained:

> Cognitive dissonance is when two competing ideas conflict…It's difficult to look at someone like [John] MacArthur, whom one would have respected, and understand that something isn't quite right here. And so most people are not comfortable in the point of cognitive dissonance. And so, you have one of two options in anything that is cognitively dissonant. One is to say, "Well, that can't possibly be true."…The other option is to say, "Well, I don't quite understand it. It doesn't quite line up, but I need to look at that." Most

---

[2] Grace to You, "Thinking Biblically About the COVID-19 Pandemic: An Interview with John MacArthur." Retrieved from YouTube.

people aren't willing to do that. Because there's a lot of sacrifice that's involved in the second choice…I think that's why people will stand up and try to revise the history. Because they're not comfortable with that point of cognitive dissonance.

To be fair, MacArthur and the elders of Grace Community Church did not deny suspending the assembly of the saints[3] for multiple weeks – but that only makes the revisionist history by this pastor more striking. At the same time, it is somewhat under-standable. Grace Community Church *eventually* did reopen, and *then* the church's marketing team chose to present that reopening as a faithful stand against governmental tyranny. The narrative put forth – complete with a feature length documentary[4] – was that Grace Community Church was an example of faithfulness and boldness during Covid-19.

But MacArthur and the church elders *never* repented of suspending worship. So, perhaps people just want a hero. Facts be damned. "They never shut down."

---

[3] Their proffered excuses for such an abandonment of the Christian assembly will be examined in Chapter 3, as well as the revisionist history they involved themselves in.

[4] In 2023, a documentary entitled *The Essential Church* was released. The film highlights Grace Church's legal battles over reconvening the assembly *after* shutting it down for months. Promotional material for the film said, "When governments use Covid edicts to restrict the gathering and worship of the Church, three pastors facing the risk of imprisonment re-open their churches in the face of a world that has chosen to comply." The great irony is that those *three churches* also chose to *comply* when they initially *shut down*, and, as far as I know, never openly *repented* of shutting down. The film should have been about the churches that never shut down.

A FAULTY FOUNDATION

Many pastors were completely frazzled by the government lockdown orders in 2020. They had long imbibed the John MacArthur "easy call" mentality when it came to submitting to Caesar. Years and years of two-kingdom theology, relegating the claims of Christ to personal religiosity, and treating Christians who sought to apply God's Law-Word to the civil sphere like pariahs, did not provide American pastors with the necessary spiritual and theological capital to stand up against Anthony Fauci and state governors.

Nevertheless, many church leaders knew something *seemed* wrong with the shutdown orders in March 2020. But they still acquiesced to the government. To justify that decision, they looked at the crowd. I personally heard from multiple pastors who said that part of their decision to cancel the assembly of the saints was based on the fact that *most* of the churches in their area had shut down. They found comfort in the multitude. More comfort should have been found in the Word of God: "Thou shalt not follow a multitude to do evil, neither agree in a controversy to decline after many and overthrow the truth" (Exodus 23:2). Instead of first looking to the Bible, and then to the faithful example of Christians throughout church history, most evangelical and Reformed pastors looked to the practice of their peers (their multitude of counselors) – peers who acted like the rest of the world.

The closing of the American church, especially the Reformed assemblies, was a display of worldliness. It contradicted all the books about Christian faithfulness by Reformed pastors, all the conferences about being a light in the world, and all the sermons about the importance of the assembly of the saints. It was completely at odds with the Bible and the godly example of our spiritual forebears. One begins to understand, then, the cognitive dissonance that pastors who shut down their churches along with MacArthur still have to this day. Perhaps a nagging conscience is at play, given that these church leaders have generally exhibited *no repentance* concerning the cancelling of the assembly. If these men would *confess* their sins, they could enjoy a clear conscience (cf. 1 John 1:9).

TRUTH MATTERS

God desires "truth in the inward parts" (Psalm 51:6, NKJV). Certainly, then, he also desires truth in the "outward parts." To believe falsehoods, such as Grace Community Church "never shut down," or to promote such churches – which exhibited no repentance after shutting down – as models of faithfulness is unhelpful. It is not the truth.

Another falsehood that spread during the early months of the lockdowns (and to this day) is that *every* American church shut down in 2020. This is simply not true. It is convenient, however, to make that claim. It provides cover for those churches that *did* shut down, expressed *no* repentance over that decision, and then later presented themselves as models of *boldness* (e.g., Grace Community Church in

California). If everyone was doing it, maybe it was not that bad. However, God keeps a faithful remnant, even amid great apostasy. So, if only *one* American church remained faithful during Covid-19 – *that* is the church worthy of imitation. As John Knox said, "A man with God is always in the majority." So too is a church with God.

A SEQUEL

My personal experience is not overly special, but I will document it here for context. When Covid-19 came along in the spring of 2020, I (like hundreds of ordinary Christians in America) never hesitated for a moment to meet with believers in Christ (without a mask and with no social distancing). Nor did I hesitate to call on church leaders to refuse to cancel the assembly of the saints. The Delaware church I was attending at the time, however, suspended the assembly of the saints, forcing me and a few families to assemble without the sanction of our church leaders. We would meet in the driveway of a man's home (not my choice to be outside) and then I would invite several families over to my home for fellowship and food every Lord's Day. Those meals were wonderful times of fellowship – no masks, no distancing. (Among our number was a nurse working at a local hospital.) I remember my pastor calling me on the phone and expressing concern that our physical gatherings on Sunday mornings might distract us from "worshipping" with the church virtually via an online video. I was not persuaded, and

I would later find out that he was recording his sermons on Saturday, and speaking during those recordings as if it were Sunday. It was a charade and a ruse.

On April 12, 2020, during one of those off-the-grid, in-person gatherings on Sunday morning, when my pastor *should* have been leading the church, I preached a sermon entitled, "Doing as He Did Aforetime: Unprecedented Times Call for Precedented Measures."[5] In that sermon, I looked to the example of Daniel and argued for consistent faithfulness, regardless of government edicts or potential risks. By the next month, I had turned that sermon into a book, *Essential Service: Coronavirus and the Assembly of the Saints*. In the foreword to that book, Jon Speed wrote:

> I have lost faith in the evangelical gatekeepers. The book reviewers. The conference speakers. The bestselling authors. The men who tell us how we ought to respond to cultural trends and whose writings get passed around amongst pastors like baseball trading cards used to get passed around in elementary school…When the coronavirus fell upon the United States, the gatekeepers advised the rest of us small fry to fall into our places in the parade away from the Lord's Day assembly. The threat of disease and death, the wisdom of pundits, and the guiding hand of government seemed to have more influence than the words of Scripture and the examples of church history. It almost seemed as if the teaching

---

[5] Audio of that sermon is available by visiting: tinyurl.com/covidsermon

about the Lord's Day assembly mysteriously disappeared from our confessions of faith, while Hebrews 10:24-25 strangely vanished from our Bibles. While I am sure that the response of most leaders was based on a pure motive, the result has been to add confusion to calamity. Take away the Lord's Day from the church, John Owen wrote, and "neglect and confusion will quickly cast out all regard unto solemn worship."

Indeed, the gatekeepers (the celebrity pastors, seminary graduates, and cautious elder boards) essentially told faithful Christians to pound sand. *The church is closed; you're on your own.*

I shared my thoughts, and my book, with my pastor and elders in Delaware. I said the church should *never* stop meeting. For example, I wrote the following in *Essential Service* in 2020:

> While there are many circumstances which would cause Christians to relocate their assembly and change meeting times, *no threat should be able to cancel such physical meetings.* Even in the case of inclement weather, cancelling the service for the *entire* congregation seems to be an act that should be reserved for each individual Christian. Surely many Christians in other nations risk far more in meeting with God's people on a sunny day than we do when there is snow on the road. None of this is to minimize our concern to prevent bodily harm, either to ourselves or others, but it is to put such concerns in their proper place (see Matthew 10:28).[6]

---

[6] *Essential Service: Coronavirus and the Assembly of the Saints* (2020), p. 95.

At the time (early 2020), I did not argue with the claims that the coronavirus was a seriously deadly virus. I had my doubts even then, but my point stood *regardless* of that – namely, the church should keep meeting *even if* a deadly virus is present. I also wrote:

> While the benefits to gathering as God's people are primarily spiritual benefits – related to fighting sin and apostasy – such gatherings also benefit our whole being...A joyful heart is the product of faith in God. Charles Spurgeon recognized this truth during a time of contagious illness in England: 'Faith by cheering the heart keeps it free from the fear which, in times of pestilence, kills more than the plague itself.' ... Faith in God is strengthened when the saints gather together. Meeting together, therefore, provides not only spiritual benefits, but also physical benefits. Individual Christians may choose to stay home during the coronavirus (or any other type of crisis). They may also choose to wear a mask or a hazmat suit. But such *personal decisions* should not be applied to an entire congregation, effectively eliminating the ability of all Christians to avail themselves of one of the greatest means of spiritual and physical strengthening.[7]

My concerns fell on deaf ears. The church remained closed, only opening many weeks later with social distancing and face mask requirements. And – just as in the case of MacArthur and Grace Community Church – there was *no* public repentance and *no*

---

[7] *Essential Service: Coronavirus and the Assembly of the Saints* (2020), p. 40-41.

apology for suspending the assembly of the saints in the first place. I could not abide such compromise and lack of repentance from men who were supposed to be examples of Christian faithfulness to me and my family. I resigned my membership shortly thereafter.

I kept trying to meet with whomever desired to be free from man-made regulations and edicts concerning the assembly of the saints. (Unfortunately, some of the men went back to churches which had previously closed their doors on the saints.) I made my book available for free online, in the hopes of encouraging other Christians.[8] I soon began receiving e-mail messages about my book. I was overwhelmed with the response to *Essential Service* – a self-published book, written by a nobody without an assembly to meet with (other than a few faithful brothers at the time). For the sake of space, I will only share a segment of one e-mail, received nearly two years after the book was first published:

> Your book came at a perfect time. I won't go into details about how we see God's hand in timing but please know it is being used and it's very timely…I am in Western Australia, the last place on earth to get covid in community as the state had been locked down for the better part of 2 years. Being the last place on earth with

[8] You can acquire a free PDF of *Essential Service: Coronavirus and the Assembly of the Saints* by visiting https://essentialservice.dudaone.com. Paperback copies are available for purchase via Amazon. Several months after I published *Essential Service*, another book, *Coronavirus and the Leadership of the Christian Church: A Sacred Trust Broken* was published (in October of 2020). That book, written by Ernest Springer, Joel Yeager, and Daniel O'Roark, provides a much more in-depth analysis than I provide in *Essential Service*.

tyrannical mandates, seeing how ineffective they were in [the] rest of the world, would make us think that as a church we too would learn from what has gone over in [the] rest of world, particularly churches. But alas no, mostly I think because of the $250,000 fine attached to those caught not wearing a mask in a building, our leadership came down very strong. Basically, as we said [we] couldn't wear a mask in worship (or anywhere else for me) we were unwelcome for 2.5 months. A month ago we had a congregational meeting, and there was so much in there that was wrong, that we really doubt the future of this church. A number of us feel that we need to write, addressing all these wrongs, and finding your book this week, this day, can only be from God. It [summarizes] everything we want to say.[9]

I received numerous messages like that one, several from overseas.[10] Unfortunately, the broader American church and her leaders did not repent of the suspension of the assembly of the saints.

In *Essential Service*, I tried to write with excessive charity – in hindsight, perhaps the greatest flaw of the book was such an approach. Though I clearly argued against ever shutting down the assembly of the saints, I tried to rely on persuasive arguments and examples to make the case, rather than explicitly appealing to the pastor's *duty* to meet with his sheep. I was hoping that people – especially my elders – would respond to a reasoned, charitable articulation of why the

---

[9] Excerpted from e-mails sent to the author on June 15, 2022.
[10] See Appendix B for more.

assembly of the saints was beneficial and should *never* be suspended. They didn't. And I too, like Jon Speed, lost any remaining faith I might have had in the "evangelical gatekeepers."

This book, therefore, is not coming from a place of hopeful anticipation in the evangelical gatekeepers. It is an indictment and a jeremiad. It pulls no punches, but "faithful are the wounds of a friend [and] profuse are the kisses of an enemy" (Proverbs 27:6, ESV). It fills in what was missing from *Essential Service*, not in terms of a new theological position, but in terms of a more direct approach. Truly, if a pastor is not *required* to assemble with his sheep, this book is futile. If danger, sickness, persecution, or government mandates can override the pastor's responsibility to gather with the flock, then this book is to be more pitied than all books.

However, I believe God will not allow truly regenerate pastors to be comfortable with such a low view of their duty. This is why the issue of cancelling the assembly was, and remains, a hot-button topic. The regenerate pastors *know* it was wrong, and are, at some level, convicted. Thus, they continue to grasp for justifications for their actions when confronted. My hope is that writing frankly about the dereliction of their duty will bring these men to the glorious place of humble repentance. Martin Luther once said, "Wounds cannot be healed until they are revealed, and sins cannot be forgiven until they are confessed." Unless the shepherds who scattered the sheep own their actions as *sinful*, they will not find healing.

Indeed, if pastors who cancelled the assembly of the saints will openly repent, they should be restored in the American mind. Sadly, the spiritual health of the church is such that many parishioners think their elders did no wrong in suspending the assembly. But many do know better. The frustration of level-headed Christians against totalitarian bureaucrats at Fauci's beck and call is also rightly directed towards pastors who did the evil one's work by scattering the sheep. They scattered the sheep by suspending the assembly of the saints. Jeremiah's indictment levied against the false shepherds in his day applies to them: "Woe be unto the pastors that destroy and scatter the sheep of my pasture" (Jeremiah 23:1).

I don't presume to have a special qualification or status to make this indictment. I make it because it is the truth. The professing Reformed church, by and large, has been a failure in my lifetime, and the Covid-19 debacle is one of the clearest examples of that. For the sake of my sanity, for the sake of those who want to accurately remember what our evangelical leaders did during 2020, and for the sake of my children after me – I submit this book for the historical record and for the consideration of every thoughtful person left in America. May God be pleased to strengthen the shepherds, so that they never again scatter the sheep.

1

THE SHEPHERD'S DUTY

A good shepherd never abandons his sheep. He will even lay down his life for them. The hireling, on the other hand, flees when danger arises – danger to *himself* or danger to *his sheep* – because he "careth not for the sheep" (John 10:13). A Christian pastor is called to be a good shepherd to God's people. Peter put it like this:

> The Elders which are among you, I beseech which am also an Elder, and a witness of the sufferings of Christ, and also a partaker of the glory that shall be revealed, *Feed the flock of God*, which dependeth upon you, caring for it not by constraint, but willingly: not for filthy lucre, but of a ready mind: Not as though ye were Lords over God's heritage, but that ye may be examples to the flock. (1 Peter 5:1-3)

Can you imagine a shepherd who would turn away his sheep, coming to him to be fed? Can you imagine a pastor who would turn away his people, coming to him to be nourished by God's Word and the fellowship of the saints? Can you imagine a pastor who would tell his parishioners to stay away from their shepherd and their fellow believers? Can you imagine a *pastor* who *scatters* the sheep? Prior to 2020, such a scenario would have been hard to imagine for many Reformed and evangelical churchmen – men who had previously exhorted congregants about the importance of meeting with the local church. But that nightmare became a reality for thousands of Christians during the worldly paranoia surrounding Covid-19: The shepherds shut the sheep out of the assembly. The shepherds scattered the sheep.

Central to a proper response to temptations to cancel the assembly of the saints is a biblical understanding of both the pastor's role and the importance of the fellowship of the saints. To begin with, the Bible commands us to gather together with fellow believers in the local assembly:

> And let us consider how to stir up one another to love and good works, not neglecting to meet together, as is the habit of some, but encouraging one another, and all the more as you see the Day drawing near. (Hebrews 10:24-25, ESV).

John Gill, commenting on this passage, noted:

> It is the duty of saints to assemble together for public worship, on the account of God, who has appointed it, who approves of it, and whose glory is concerned in it;

and on the account of the saints themselves, that they may be delighted, refreshed, comforted, instructed, edified, and perfected; and on account of others, that they may be convinced, converted, and brought to the knowledge and faith of Christ; and in imitation of the primitive saints.

As Gill notes, there are numerous benefits to assembling, both for the "saints themselves" and for "others." Pastors who cancelled the assembly of the saint were effectively preventing the saints from those benefits in the name of *potential* harm that *could* come to someone if he freely chose to assemble with his spiritual family on the Lord's Day.[1] They also robbed the watching world of an example of a people who do not fear death – an example desperately needed as the masses succumbed to fear and paranoia.

The assembly of the saints is all at once a responsibility, a privilege, and a great source of comfort and help for the saint. The gathering together of Christians is not something a pastor or elder board has the authority to cancel. People are free to assemble together, especially Christian people desirous of spiritual encouragement (cf. Romans 1:11-12).

PASTORS AS NANNIES

The justification proffered for closing church was that meeting with the sheep could lead to harm for

---

[1] I refer the reader to Chapter 2 of *Essential Service* for more on the benefits (both spiritual and physical) of the assembly of the saints.

the sheep. Pastors adopted a nanny mentality[2] and claimed to shut down the assembly of the saints for the "safety" of the sheep. *"I'm willing to sacrifice myself for you, but I will not allow you to put me in that situation. Nor will I allow you to make up your own mind about the value of spiritual good in the face of potential harm."* This was a powerplay for *more* authority as a pastor. Here's why: The Bible does not provide a pastor with the authority to tell parishioners when it is safe to leave home.

The pastor's job is to walk in holiness, gather with the sheep, and feed them with the Word of God. Implicitly placing people on house arrest or hiding behind locked church doors is not part of the pastor's job. Just as there are limits to familial and governmental authority, so too are their limits to pastoral authority. Christians would rightly reject a pastor who would attempt to use his authority to forbid church members from driving to the grocery store or hospital during a snowstorm, and yet many embraced the supposed authority of pastors to tell their sheep that they were *not allowed* to gather with their shepherd and fellow sheep. A Christian pastor has not been granted nanny-level authority by Christ – he does not have authority to direct every detail of the sheep's lives. Nor does he have the authority to tell the sheep they cannot congregate,[3] but this

---

[2] Much like our civil government did during 2020. See my book, *Seven Statist Sins: The Capital Vices Civil Government in American Society* for more.

[3] If a pastor retorts, "They are free to congregate on the Lord's Day, but I will not be there – for *their* safety, of course," then he is revealing his own fear and lack of concern for his sheep. He is not worthy of being a

authority was assumed by many pastors. The pastors either played the tyrant and told congregants they were not allowed to have their own gatherings or played the nanny and made decisions for the people, preventing them from gathering with their shepherd and brethren in Christ.

At the root of proffered justifications for cancelling church is an assumed pastoral responsibility for making choices on behalf of parishioners concerning their physical safety. This faulty assumption leads pastors to shoulder an impossible and unbiblical burden of weighing risk every week. The reasoning of these pastors is as follows: Once the level of perceived risk for gathering as a church reaches a *certain level,* then any physical harm that follows is the *fault* of the pastor(s) for not cancelling the assembly. In fact, one pastor told me that *blood would have been on his hands* if even one person died due to his willingness to gather with the sheep. We could illustrate this mindset as follows:

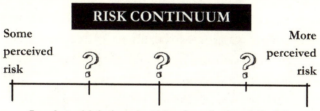

RISK CONTINUUM

Some perceived risk   More perceived risk

Level at which there is "blood on the hands" of the pastor(s) if someone dies in the course of gathering with his spiritual family.

---

shepherd. (In Chapter 3, I will address the oft-raised objection: "But what about cancelling the assembly for a blizzard?")

Undoubtedly, there is always *some level* of risk whenever anyone steps out his door (or gets out of bed for that matter…or decides to *stay* in bed). As Bilbo said, "It's a dangerous business, Frodo, going out your door." Indeed, it is, and we must add to the normal risk of everyday living the persecution Christians face for their faith. Jesus told his followers, "If they have persecuted me, they will persecute you also,"[4] and we are urged to not fear death in the course of our Christian walk.[5]

Nevertheless, the nanny-mentality of many pastors causes them to grasp for control over risk. However, these pastors are unable to define (biblically or logically) *two* key things. First, they cannot consistently define *where* on the continuum the responsibility shifts from the individual parishioner to the pastor. Second, they cannot define *why* (at *any* point on the continuum) they are responsible for the choices of others and thus have the authority to limit the choices of faithful saints. Furthermore, we could hope many of these pastors would be honest enough to admit that they were duped by a media-induced, government-supported narrative concerning Covid-19 that played on the fear of death. Christians should have demonstrated a different spirit, but such an opportunity was squelched by pastors cancelling church under the auspices of risk analysis.

---

[4] John 15:20.

[5] "Fear them not therefore: for there is nothing covered, that shall not be disclosed, nor hid, that shall not be known…And fear ye not them which kill the body, but are not able to kill the soul: but rather fear him, which is able to destroy both soul and body in hell" (Matthew 10:26, 28).

The "blood on my hands" mentality is at home in an atomistic, materialistic society obsessed with blame, narcissism, and safety. The idea that the overriding metric by which to live is risk analysis is fitting for a people with no grasp of spiritual realities. If our physical wellbeing is more important than our spiritual wellbeing, then the assembly of the saints should be cancelled often, and Jesus' words about not fearing death or physical persecution fall flat. But such is not the case, and the weighty exhortations in Scripture that call us to love not our lives even unto death are not meant to be relegated to an elder board who will decide when the risk is "worth" it for the peons in the pews.

Another point missed by many pastors is that great spiritual harm follows when a pastor goes beyond his Christ-ordained authority. First, harm comes to the pastor. A pastor is charged with keeping watch over the souls of those in his care.[6] The rest is not his purview. When a pastor shoulders the excess burden of being responsible for the *decisions* of parishioners, made in the *liberty* of the Christian conscience and in accord with their duty to gather with their spiritual family, he is shouldering a weight he cannot bear. Pastors shoulder the legitimate burden of caring for the souls of the people. To add to that duty a man-made and illegitimate burden is, intentional or not, a prideful usurpation of what does not belong to the pastor. It is inevitable that such a usurpation will result in a needless toll on the pastor's

---

[6] Hebrews 13:17.

psyche. Men are not meant to sustain such things. Even worse than the strain this illegitimate burden brings is the fact that it will inevitably lead the pastor to *sin* by "domineering over those in [his] charge."[7]

When a pastor oversteps his bounds and uses his authority to forbid the obedience of the sheep in gathering together, a real offense has occurred. On the other hand, the vague, nanny-inspired idea of having "blood on our hands" for Christians dying because they chose to obey God at risk to their own safety is not a real offense. It is a man-made tradition. It cannot be defended from the Bible. These pastors are binding heavy burdens, hard to bear, and laying them on their *own* shoulders (and the shoulders of their fellow elders). If pastors who scattered the sheep would repent, not only would the church be strengthened, but these men would be eased of a man-made burden and find freedom in leading God's people as a bold example, not as a calculating risk analyst.

A pastor will *not* give an account for the risks people in his congregation took; he will give an account for his faithfulness (or lack thereof) to what God has clearly called him to do. As Charles Spurgeon said, "When we know our duty, first thoughts are always best; if the thing is obviously

---

[7] 1 Peter 5:3, ESV. It is noteworthy that Peter juxtaposes domineering (or lording it over) the people with the pastor's duty to set an *example*. This example-setting is the pastor's duty as it concerns obedience in the face of death. He is to simply set an example of courageousness, and then be patient and gentle with those who might not have the strength of faith to stand boldly. He is not to make decisions for other people.

right, never think about it a second time, but straightway go and do it." Nanny-mentality pastors are caught in a complex web of man-made burdens, unbiblical blame-bearing, and infinite second guessing. For a pastor to assume such an unbiblical responsibility will necessarily require him to assume unbiblical authority – namely, the supposed authority to cancel the assembly of the saints for all the sheep when he (or the elder board) deems the risk of assembling just "too high." Christ has not granted such authority to pastors. Pastors are given authority to "feed the flock of God"[8] and "watch for your souls."[9] Pastors are *not* given the authority to prevent the saints from obeying the Bible – in this case, "the assembling of ourselves together."[10]

When a pastor goes beyond his Christ-ordained authority, harm also comes to his people. Specifically, by depriving *every single parishioner* of a shepherd willing to gather with his spiritual family, the nanny-pastor is preventing the sheep from the ability to demonstrate faith in the face of fear and enjoy the soul-sustaining benefits of gathering with their spiritual family. As I argued in *Essential Service*, there are also physical benefits of obedience in the face of death. In fact, it has been argued that given the communal nature of man and the psychological damage that isolation brings, the nearly nation-wide cancellation of church did far *more* damage (spiritual *and* physical) than

---

[8] 1 Peter 5:2.
[9] Hebrews 13:17.
[10] Hebrews 10:25, KJV.

Covid-19 did, a virus with an incredibly low death rate.[11] Be that as it may, it is not the job of the pastor to endlessly add new metrics to his analysis concerning gathering with the sheep. His job is to be faithful and stay in his lane.

I spoke with one pastor who said that after closing down, and then requiring masks for the first Sunday back, only two people left permanently.[12] This high percentage of parishioners who stayed was appealed to as anecdotal evidence that shutting down the church did not harm the people. The two people that left were specifically described as no longer walking with the Lord – an apparent attempt to minimize the seriousness of their departure, as if the departure of *faithful* saints would have been weightier. However, assuming this pastor was shepherding properly, the two departed parishioners only exhibited such apostasy *after* the church shut down. In that case, their departures, and subsequent falling away, could be more logically appealed to as an example of the dangers of cancelling the assembly of the saints, a danger perhaps most applicable to those weak in faith. After all, the warning immediately following the charge in Hebrews 10:25 to not forsake the assembly relates to *apostasy* – the very thing this pastor said had

---

[11] According to 2020 data from England and Wales, approximately 0.016% of the population died due to Covid-19 with no pre-existing conditions. The percent drops even lower when considering age. Among a population of over 59 million people, only 1,557 people under the age of 65 died due to Covid-19 with no pre-existing conditions.

[12] Others left initially but returned later. The appeal to church attendance remaining stable after pastors scattered the sheep will be addressed in the conclusion of this book.

happened.

These pastors also deprived their people of the liberty to obey God in the face of danger. If a parishioner dies because he wanted to gather with his spiritual family, in the face of either a supposedly deadly virus or a violent jihadist group in Burkina Faso, that *parishioner* will give an account to God for his actions. The pastor will not be held responsible for the convictions and faithfulness of that parishioner. In truth, such a parishioner may end up receiving a far greater reward than any cautious pastor ever will. For a pastor to do anything other than commit to being available every Lord's Day for his people is to defraud them of the opportunity to stand with their Christian family.

The Bible simply does not authorize the pastor to decide *if* he will meet with his sheep. If a pastor is unwilling to gather with his sheep weekly (not simply on a one-on-one basis, but with however many of them are willing to gather), no matter the risk, he ought to hang up his pastoral spikes and leave the task to men – namely, godly pastors who will set an example of courage in the face of death.

ONE-ON-ONE MEETINGS?

Some pastors argued that *they* were still fulfilling *their* pastoral duties by meeting one-on-one with some parishioners. However, this is inadequate for at least two reasons. First, it is unlikely that the pastor met with every single member of his flock every week on a one-on-one basis. Second, and more importantly, by suspending the *assembly*, the pastors *prevented* the congregants from the ability to experience the comfort, edification, and spiritual sustenance that is provided in fellowshipping with the body. The pastor is unable to provide what only the assembly can provide. Unsurprisingly, pastors played up the importance of *their* one-on-one pastoral "duties," while downplaying the wider duty and responsibility that falls on *all believers* to meet with the church. For a pastor to focus on *his personal duties*, while simultaneously preventing the sheep from gathering as an assembly – something many of the sheep will also be convinced is *their* duty as members of the body – is selfish.

If a pastor, unwilling to meet with the flock due to perceived risk, appeals to his meeting one-on-one as a *substitute* for his willingness to gather with the assembled body, he will have to deal with his own standard. Namely, his claims that he would be responsible if someone contracts a disease and dies *because* he did not cancel the assembly of the saints, also applies to anyone contracting a deadly disease *because* the pastor met one-on-one and spread a virus in that manner. Blood would also be on his hands, according to his logic, in that case.

'WE DIE AT OUR POSTS'

The duty of a pastor includes the duty to *never abandon his sheep*. The threat of death (via persecution *or* sickness) does not free a pastor from his responsibility to meet with the sheep. In the 16th century, the bubonic plague – a disease which, unlike Covid-19, had a seriously *high* death toll – hit the German city of Wittenberg, home of Martin Luther. Though it cost him dearly, Luther refused to leave, and he refused to stay away from his congregants.

> In 1527, when the bubonic plague hit Wittenberg, Martin Luther refused calls to flee the city and protect himself. Rather, he stayed and ministered to the sick. The refusal to flee cost his daughter Elizabeth her life.[13]

Luther rejected the idea that a godly pastor would abandon the sheep during a time when they most needed to learn how to live and how to die. Luther wrote:

> Those who are engaged in spiritual ministry such as preachers and pastors must likewise remain steadfast before the peril of death. We have a plain command from Christ, "A good shepherd lays down his life for the sheep but the hireling sees the wolf coming and flees." For when people are dying, they most need a spiritual ministry which strengthens and comforts their consciences by word and sacrament and in faith overcomes death.[14]

During the plague, Luther wrote a letter to answer the

[13] Lyman Stone, "Christianity Has Been Handling Epidemics for 2000 Years." Retrieved from www.foreignpolicy.com.
[14] Quoted in "Pastors and Pestilence: Martin Luther's Views on the Church, Christians, and the Black Death" by Chris Sundheim (*Historia*, 1997, Volume 6, p. 23).

question of whether it is acceptable to flee one's city during a deadly pestilence.[15] He acknowledged that fleeing was acceptable for some people, but *not* for those charged with the spiritual care of the saints. For example, he called on "those who are engaged in a spiritual ministry such as preachers and pastors [to] likewise remain steadfast before the peril of death," and only leave if there are "enough preachers …available in one locality and they agree to encourage the other clergy to leave."[16] Luther urged pastors to stand as examples of faith, and he warned of the spiritual danger present when the fear of death reigns:

> The devil is so very evil that he not only tries constantly to kill and murder but also gives vent to his spleen by making us fearful, afraid, and timid about death in order that death might appear to us to be the worst possible thing, that we might have neither rest nor peace in this life, and that we might despair of our life.[17]

Such was the case during 2020 – people were being taught that death from Covid-19 was the worst possible thing. Such spiritual harm was not

---

[15] The main question the letter addressed, therefore, was not whether the pastor should cease meeting with his people, but rather if he was justified in leaving the entire *geographical* locale. However, I believe the principles from church history (though subordinate to Scripture) are applicable in many ways. As will be argued below, after answering the question of if one may flee the city during the plague, he calls on those remaining to "attend church."

[16] Martin Luther, *Luther's Works*, Vol. 43: Devotional Writings II. Quoted from a reprint by *The Lutheran Witness* (March 2020).

[17] Ibid.

considered by pastors making calculations based on an ambiguous risk continuum.

Some have argued that even though Luther urged some pastors to stay and minister during the plague, he still cancelled the assembly of the saints. If Luther did, he erred. However, the evidence points in the other direction. For example, in the aforementioned letter, Luther offered his counsel on how people ought to conduct themselves during the plague:

> Because this letter will go out in print for people to read, I regard it useful to add some brief instructions on how one should care and provide for the soul in time of death. We have done this orally from the pulpit, and still do so every day in fulfilment of the ministry to which we have been called as pastors. First, one must admonish the people to attend church and listen to the sermon so that they learn through God's word how to live and how to die.[18]

Clearly, based on those words, Luther still called on people to assemble ("attend church"). He had also set the example of public preaching ("from the pulpit").[19] His conclusion is that the gathering of the church is a form of loving neighbor that should *continue* during the plague. Gathering with God's people, hearing the

---

[18] Ibid.

[19] Live-streaming technology had not yet been discovered in Luther's day, but he did have other means of communication (namely, letter writing) that he could have resorted to *in lieu* of the assembly of the saints if he believed such a course of action was biblical. However, he did not do that. He urged people to "attend church."

preached Word, and taking communion (the Lord's Supper) should not be suspended due to the plague.

Luther did agree that sick people could be quarantined, but he did not view the threat of a plague as a valid reason to stop meeting with his parishioners any more than he viewed the threat of persecution as a valid reason to stay away from other Christians. Chris Sundheim explains Luther's view:

> But, [Luther] wrote, an outbreak of the black death is no different from any other threat. According to Scripture, God sent four scourges: famine, sword, wild beasts, and pestilence. The Bible teaches that in each of the first three cases, devoted believers may save themselves only after they have seen to the care of others, just as Abraham, Jacob, and David did themselves. Luther expected that some Christians would doubt whether the plague could be compared to scourges described in the Bible. Biblical figures, after all, never faced the black death. "Death is death, no matter how it occurs," Luther insisted. Regardless of whether the threat is persecution or plague, Christians are bound by God's law first to meet obligations to their fellow men. Only afterwards may they think of their own escape. Those who panic and ignore this holy directive will be judged harshly in the eyes of God.[20]

If a Christian family member became infected, Luther urged that the pastor be called to provide (in-person)

---

[20] Chris Sundheim, "Pastors and Pestilence: Martin Luther's Views on the Church, Christians, and the Black Death," *Historia*, p. 24.

counseling and communion. Christians were welcomed, even encouraged, to take precautions during the plague, but that did not change Luther's responsibility. Lyman Stone summarizes the takeaway from Luther's example and exhortations:

> Luther provides a clear articulation of the Christian epidemic response: We die at our posts. Christian doctors cannot abandon their hospitals, Christian governors cannot flee their districts, Christian pastors cannot abandon their *congregations*. The plague does not dissolve our duties: It turns them to crosses, on which we must be prepared to die.[21]

However, just as in our day, many shepherds in Luther's day failed to lay down their lives for the sheep:

> [E]vidence suggests that some priests would not serve in plague-stricken areas without exceptionally high salaries. Such behavior raised obvious questions about the Church's commitment to its flock and the priests' materialism. Add to this a few notorious stories of priests abandoning their infected communities and one sees why the Church's credibility was so damaged.[22]

And just as in Luther's day, the credibility of the church was seriously damaged in 2020. As Ernest

---

[21] Lyman Stone, "Christianity Has Been Handling Epidemics for 2000 Years." Emphasis added.
[22] Sundheim, "Pastors and Pestilence: Martin Luther's Views on the Church, Christians, and the Black Death," p. 27.

Springer put it:

> [T]he credibility of the Church has been diminished if not lost altogether in the minds of some who see church leaders' support of societal panic no different than secular culture whose trust is in themselves and in government control.[23]

The Christian pastor, by virtue of his office, is called to die at his post caring for the sheep. That death could come via a bullet from a Schutzstaffel officer's gun or from a contagious virus.

Even if no one else was willing to show love and compassion to those infected with Covid-19, Christian pastors should have been willing to lay down their lives and meet with their sheep (as an *assembly*). Instead, they effectively abandoned their posts, and claimed that phone calls, Skype conferences, or one-on-one meetings sufficed in the face of what many people deemed a serious threat at the time. *They risked nothing and gained nothing.*

Many pastors, especially in affluent America, are ignorant of their responsibility to lay down their lives for the sheep. They go to seminary, study the Bible, read the theological books, and view their duty as largely esoteric. Study and prayer are important, even vital, but they are not everything. In fact, a pastor's greatest duty is to be a godly *example* to his sheep. The sheep need someone to *follow*. This is why biblical pastoral qualifications deal primarily with *character*.

---

[23] Ernest Springer, *Coronavirus and the Leadership of the Christian Church*, p. 55.

And this is why Peter wrote that pastors must "be examples to the flock" (1 Peter 5:3). A willingness to die for the sheep is a cost that every pastoral intern ought to wrestle with. *If you are not willing to sacrifice yourself for the sheep, do not become a shepherd.* This cost is more easily understood in cultures where Christians are heavily persecuted. In communist lands, when a man becomes a pastor, he knows that he is likely to be the *first* to be targeted by the godless government. Simply by serving as the pastor, he is demonstrating that he is willing to die for the sheep.

The need for pastors to be willing to lay down their lives for the sheep was evident during Covid-19, but most pastors were unwilling.[24] Here's what we need to remember: Thousands of American pastors did not simply *recommend* that the vulnerable wait it out at home – no, these pastors *absented themselves* from the assembly, they told the congregation that worship was *suspended.* The shepherds were unwilling to meet with the sheep. In the end, fear reigned.

In the following chapter we will look at some (disappointing) church announcements from 2020, but an announcement with the following spirit is what every faithful pastor *should* have declared the moment the lockdown orders (or suggestions) were released:

I am your pastor. I have counted the cost and accepted the call to lay down my life for you. Just as a good doctor

---

[24] The need for this willingness was *revealed* even though Covid-19 was not an overly dangerous contagion. However, because some pastors *thought* Covid-19 was potentially deadly, the ordeal revealed their unwillingness to gather with the sheep if they *thought* it might cost them their lives.

would not leave the sick to die alone, I will not leave you alone. I will never cancel the assembly of the saints for risks to my own safety. Nor will I sit in judgment on your conscience or tell you when it is safe to leave your home. I will continue to lead the sheep in corporate worship. We'll meet in our building until we are forcibly removed. Then we will meet outside. But we will keep on meeting. Until I am locked in prison, I will meet with my sheep (even then, if they let you come to me, I will not turn you away). In the snow, in the rain, in the heat, in the wind. I will be there. In person. Just as I will never cease to gather with my physical family, even during a plague, so will I never cease gathering with you. I will never ask you to wear a mask, get a vaccine, or socially distance yourself from your brothers and sisters. If you deem the assembly of the saints too much of a risk to your personal safety, you will answer to God for that. You can make your own personal health choices within the liberty of the Christian conscience. But I will be here, as an example. It is my duty and my joy. Any parishioner who wants to gather with God's people will *not* be turned away. I will never turn you away. If I must, I will die at my post. So help me God.

Would to God more pastors during 2020 had true shepherd's hearts. Then the testimony of Christ's church would have shown as a bright light amid a culture of fear, paranoia, and compromise.

Sadly, most American pastors exhibited the opposite of a shepherd's heart. They followed Fauci, not Christ. Fear, not faith.[25] We will now turn to some examples of pastors scattering the sheep in 2020.

---

[25] Luther wrote: "If someone is weak and fearful, let him flee in God's name as long as he does not neglect his duty toward his neighbor but has made adequate provision for others to provide nursing care." The pastors of the churches who scattered the sheep relegated their duties as spiritual guides to the medical professionals.

2

THE SCATTERING

In A.D. 250 the Alexandrian Plague led the pagans to "thrust aside anyone who began to be sick, and [keep] aloof even from their dearest friends."[1] The Christians, however, exhibited a different spirit (and different actions). They refused to keep themselves aloof (social distancing) from the sick (to say nothing of the healthy), and Bishop Dionysius wrote that the Christians "did not spare themselves, but kept by each other, and visited the sick without thought of their own peril, and ministered to them assiduously and treated them for their healing in Christ."[2] Some did die, but Dionysius adds that they died "joyfully." Such examples abound in Christian history, and pastors knew these stories very well. Then along came Covid-19. When the coronavirus came in March of 2020, most church leaders disregarded the bold examples of faithful Christians throughout church history. They suspended the assembly of the saints.

---

[1] *Works of Dionysius*, Epistle 12.5.

[2] *Works of Dionysius*, Epistle 12.4.

They scattered the sheep.

Many of these men were well-known pastors or teachers within the Reformed or Calvinistic tradition. Men like Joel Beeke, W. Robert Godfrey, and John MacArthur. These men cancelled church. In some cases, pastors even shut people out of the Lord's Table.[3] I cannot provide anecdotes for every church that shut down and every church that remained open. Those shepherds who scattered the sheep know who they are. There are three categories of church leaders as it concerns this topic:

1. Church leaders that did cancel the assembly of the saints, and then reopened later (whether four weeks or four months later) and yet did *not* openly repent – men like John MacArthur, W. Robert Godfrey, and Joel Beeke, among many others. They are the focus of the indictments in this book.

2. Church leaders that did cancel the assembly of the saints and/or required masks or social distancing, but openly and publicly repented of such actions and changed course. Praise God for them.[4]

---

[3] In addition to cancelling, in many cases, the Lord's Supper, some pastors required masks to take communion, effectively excommunicating anyone who would not buy the narrative and put on a face mask when gathering with their spiritual family. I will explore this further below.

[4] For example, Joel Saint recounted how his assembly (Independence Reformed Bible Church in Lancaster County, Pennsylvania) was told they could no longer use the school they rented for church services on Sunday mornings during Covid-19. After a week or two, the church began meeting

3. Church leaders that never cancelled the assembly of the saints and did *not* require masks or social distancing. No repentance needed there.

CHURCHES ACTING LIKE THE WORLD

We will first consider several examples of Category 1 church leaders – men who shut down the church and, to my knowledge, never repented (i.e., said it was *wrong* to have done so and openly committed to never doing it again).

Heritage Reformed Congregation of Grand Rapids (Michigan)
Heritage Reformed Congregation of Grand Rapids in Michigan, where Joel Beeke served as a pastor during 2020, issued a statement on March 13, 2020. Portions of it are as follows:

> The times in which we live, call for steady trust in God's sovereignty and goodness…Perhaps the greatest challenge facing us as Christians is that of fear, rather than disease. But we need to remind ourselves from the

---

at a private pavilion. Regarding the church's one or two weeks (he could not recall which it was) of not meeting in person, Saint said: "I think it was wrong. I believe we should not have done that…Whether we did it once or twice, it was wrong" (*The Lancaster Patriot Podcast,* Episode 79). Saint said they should have simply "found a tree" somewhere to meet under like the Scottish Covenanters. If Saint had not been barred from using his typical meeting place, I tend to think that he would not have missed a *single* week. However, even though he was kicked out of his meeting place against his will, he was *still* willing to admit the church should have kept meeting. That mindset is absent from men like MacArthur, who had their own church buildings to use and still cancelled the gathering of God's people. Of course, Independence Reformed Bible Church *never* required or recommended masks or social distancing.

words of Psalm 56:3, "What time I am afraid, I will trust in thee." Even in times like these. This truth will help us transform this situation from one of rampant fear into steady faith, from greedy hoarding into generous compassion, from love of self into love of neighbor, from crippling silence to a powerful witness of the gospel.

The consistory also faces the challenge of leading wisely in times like this…As leadership we are attempting to balance the honor and respect we owe to those in authority over us, as well as love for our neighbors in mitigating the risk of disease for the elderly and weak. In doing so, the executive of consistory, in consultation with medical professionals in the congregation, has taken the decision to postpone communion for the next several weeks and reduce attendance at services. We recognize this is a disappointment for the pastors, the consistory and no doubt for those who are eagerly anticipating communion this Lord's Day. Church will remain open for services this Lord's Day for those who need to be there in order to ensure that the services can be livestreamed, such as the pastors, consistory, sound technicians, and organist for both services. In order to put this in context, Governor Whitmer's executive order as of Friday, March 13, 2020, states that gatherings of over 250 people are banned and a violation of that order is considered a misdemeanor.

The statement twists language to make it appear that the church worship was not shut down. They simply wanted to "reduce" the number of sheep welcome. After all, the statement says, "Church will remain open for services this Lord's Day." But it adds this important clause: "for those who need to be there in order to ensure that the services can be livestreamed." This was a shutting out of the sheep. Only a select few were allowed to gather with the shepherd. If you were not part of that exclusive group, it was too bad for you. It was a demonstration of partiality, and the Bible says, "My brethren, do not hold the faith of our Lord Jesus Christ, the Lord of glory, with partiality."[5] The added "context" – namely, that gathering as a church would violate an executive order – demonstrates an apparent unwillingness to obey God if it means disobeying man.

The words about a "powerful witness" are revealed to be empty and insipid as they are followed by partiality and kowtowing to statist rulers. The church leaders shut the sheep out of the assembly – only an elite few had access. Note, as well, the reference to the "elderly and weak." Once again, the nanny-mentality is evident. The elderly and weak would have been free to stay home without Beeke and the other leaders preventing nearly everyone (many who were young and healthy) from gathering.

Grace Community Church (Sun Valley, California)
John MacArthur, pastor/teacher of Grace Community Church (known hereafter as Grace Church), said the following in the spring of 2020

---

[5] James 2:1, NKJV.

when government shut down orders were released: "The clear demand of Scripture is to be subject to the [civil government] … We conform, we are submissive to the government. That was an easy call for us."[6] And, naturally, Grace Church suspended services immediately. A statement later released on the church's website from MacArthur said: "Grace Church's elders decided to suspend public services while we continued live-streaming sermons from the pulpit in the Worship Center auditorium." Yes, MacArthur stayed behind the pulpit to livestream sermons, but he and his fellow elders issued a public statement saying the church suspended worship. It was a clear message to the sheep: *Stay away*. Hundreds and hundreds of congregants were kept from gathering with their shepherd and with one another.[7] Who prevented them from doing so? Their own shepherds.

Westminster Presbyterian Church (Lancaster, Pennsylvania)
Westminster Presbyterian Church is probably the largest Reformed church in Lancaster County, Pennsylvania. Throughout the years, the church has held various Ligonier Ministries conferences and events. For example, in 2016, Ligonier held their

---

[6] Grace to You, "Thinking Biblically About the COVID-19 Pandemic: An Interview with John MacArthur." Retrieved from YouTube.

[7] It is shocking to me that now, three years later, people are claiming that a church did not "shut down" if the pastor livestreamed the service. The *assembly* of the saints requires the saints to *assemble*. As mentioned above concerning Heritage Reformed Congregation of Grand Rapids, shutting out some of the sheep and letting in a select few (in order to "livestream" the service) is still effectively cancelling the assembly of the saints.

Regional Conference in conjunction with Westminster Presbyterian Church. The church has a rich history of biblical and Reformed theology, and no doubt lauded the courageous Reformers who were willing to die for the sake of the gospel. When Covid-19 hit, however, they shut their doors like many other churches. On March 20, 2020, the church sent out an e-mail stating:

> Worship Services on March 22 & 29 are cancelled. Listen or watch the livestream service at 11 am at www.westpca.com/listen or on the church app under the "Look & Listen" tab. You can follow along with a Worship Guide which includes all hymns (used by permission from Trinity Hymnal).

Several weeks later, with the church still closed, a five-page letter from Senior Pastor Chris Walker was published. In the letter, Walker wrote that while he had anticipated a "short break" from normal life and worship, the time had lengthened and some were "wondering why we continue to hold off gathering together for worship, feeling that we are disobeying Scripture." He added:

> At the heart of the questions we face as Christians is this dilemma: Gathering together for worship and fellowship is a command for God's people and is the core of our identity as the church; and yet, gathering together is what risks harm to ourselves and to our community by the unintentional spread of a new, highly contagious virus.

How do we navigate this dilemma biblically?[8]

These three churches are demonstrative of thousands of churches across the nation that closed their doors on the saints.

AN EXAMPLE OF REPENTANCE

I believe there is more than one example of pastoral repentance over the Covid-19 church closures, but I will simply list one here.

Before I do, however, a word about repentance is needed. Some have suggested that a pastor "repents" concerning his decision to close church when he says, "They fooled us once, but they won't do it again." Or, "In hindsight, we probably *could* have stayed open." Statements like those, and the sentiments behind them, are *not* representative of *repentance*.[9] Repentance involves a sense of personal wrongdoing and a brokenness over past actions. I suspect some pastors, if pressed, might offer shallow statements of pseudo-repentance (e.g., "they fooled us"). Christians must be wary of such chicanery.

Calvary Baptist Church (Natrona Heights, Pennsylvania)
Pastor Joe Jewart shut down his church in the spring of 2020. He reopened on May 24, 2020, and preached a message on the kingship of Christ. In that sermon,

---

[8] A letter to Westminster Presbyterian Church from Chris Walker provided to the author. Walker's justifications for turning away the sheep will be examined in the next chapter.

[9] Imagine the Apostle Peter, following his denial of Christ, saying, "Lord, they fooled me once, but it won't happen again." Such is not repentance.

Jewart said:

> If we are not congregating together, then there is no functioning church...So, next time our governor tells us that we cannot gather for worship, we can't obey that. We were *not courageous* enough to obey God in that sense...I wish that we had that courage, I do wish that.[10]

Jewart later released a statement summarizing his change of heart:

> I'm speaking as a pastor who sinfully complied with the humanistic government. I had the responsibility to lead the church to the throne of Christ, but instead I led them to bow before the state. Thank God for the grace found in Jesus Christ. In Him all sins are washed clean and forgotten. So, pastor, if you have taught your people to bow before the state instead of Christ by shutting down the local church that God has placed in your care, I plead with you to repent.[11]

Jewart's example is commendable. If the pastors that scattered the sheep would follow in his footsteps, it would be an important display of piety and godliness.

FAITHFUL CHURCHES
Despite the narrative, many churches *did* remain faithful to God. Many shepherds did not turn away

---

[10] Retrieved from Calvary Baptist Church's Facebook page. Emphasis added.

[11] You can read Jewart's full statement in Appendix A.

their sheep. These men – rather than men like MacArthur or Walker – are examples of fidelity that we ought to emulate and esteem. I wish I could chronicle every single faithful church, as their examples are worthy of recognition, but for the sake of space I will simply list two.

Heritage Church (Centerville, Tennessee)

Heritage Church pastor Marion Lovett had the same news media and the same Bible that Beeke, MacArthur, and Walker had, but he never shut down the assembly of the saints. When asked to explain, Lovett told me:

> We believe the Church meeting for worship is essential. We operated from presuppositions, biblical principles, and a worldview that was quite contrary to the world's and many churches at the time. Those key components directed us to apply the Word of God to our current and uncertain context at the time. It was a time of testing and we are thankful for the Lord's faithfulness in leading us.

Heritage Church never cancelled services and never required masks.[12]

---

[12] Lovett did tell me that during a couple Lord's Days in early 2020 they provided group seating for families. Lovett said, "As we gathered on the first Lord's Day of the pandemic, we cancelled all other church activities except for worship. That first Lord's Day was either Palm Sunday or Easter (I believe the former). We encouraged the people to bring lawn chairs and assemble as family units and we had an outdoor service. The next week, we were planning to do the same, but it rained, so we simply gathered into our meeting place with family groups once again, but it was back inside

By the Word Baptist Church (Azle, Texas)
Jon Speed, who wrote the foreword to *Essential Service*, served as the Pastor of Missions and Evangelism at By the Word Baptist Church during 2020. Speed told me the church never required masks or social distancing and never cancelled Sunday morning services.

Unfortunately, no documentary or biography will likely be written about Speed's faithfulness during Covid-19.

The proper response from Category 1 churches would have been to acknowledge the wisdom of Category 3 churches and openly apologize to their congregants (and the world) for their poor testimony. As stated, there was at least one example of this. However, most Category 1 churches eventually reopened, gave some excuses for closing, and moved on. In the next chapter, we will consider some of these excuses.

---

where we remained from then on. There was some mingling as to be expected, but we didn't police it."

3

THE EXCUSES

There are not many things worse than disregarding God's Word. But I can think of at least one thing worse: disregarding God's Word and then being completely oblivious to your folly. In other words, learning nothing.

The priests in Malachi's day seemed to be oblivious of their incompetence and infidelity. But they were culpable.

> A son honoreth his father, and a servant his master. If then I be a father, where is my honor? and if I be a master, where is my fear, saith the Lord of hosts unto you, O Priests that despise my Name? and ye say, Wherein have we despised thy Name? Ye offer unclean bread upon mine altar: and you say, Wherein have we polluted thee? in that ye say, The table of the Lord is not to be regarded. (Malachi 1:6-7)

The pastors in our day are not far behind in such obliviousness. In fact, they might be out in front. The great failure of the leaders of professing evangelical and Reformed churches during 2020 was that they sinned by closing their churches and preventing the saints from assembling in thousands of congregations across the nation. It was an unparalleled show of cowardice and hypocrisy.

But it gets worse.

The excuses given, the theological errors promulgated, and the narratives spun afterwards have been even more troubling than the fact that many pastors walked in fear and indecisiveness like the rest of the world for several weeks or months. The book of Hebrews instructs us: "Remember those who rule over you, who have spoken the word of God to you, whose faith follow, considering the outcome of their conduct" (Hebrews 13:7, NKJV). Godly leaders do not simply teach the word of God – that divine word leads to an "outcome," namely, a biblical way of life to be *followed*. In 2020, hundreds (probably thousands) of supposedly Reformed pastors – pastors who had previously taught that the gathering of the saints was a command by God – did not follow their own teaching. They evidenced no faith worthy of imitation.

GOD STOPPED OUR WORSHIP?

In May 2020, W. Robert Godfrey wrote in *Tabletalk* magazine: "Many Christians have expressed disappointment and frustration in the last few weeks about not being able to gather for worship because of the COVID-19 crisis. I am one of them." Godfrey went on to effectively say it was the Lord's will that churches shut their doors to the saints:

> God is sovereign over all things. "Does disaster come to a city, unless the Lord has done it?" (Amos 3:6). So He is the One who has stopped our worship as the gathered body of Christ on the Lord's Day.

According to Godfrey, it was not the cowardice or indecisiveness of church leaders that led to church closures, but *God*.

I believe in the sovereignty of God, but Godfrey's use of the doctrine is extremely poorly handled. God's sovereignty does not absolve us from our responsibility to obey him, nor does it give us license to blame him for the faithlessness of church leaders. To quote from the *Westminster Confession of Faith*, "God from all eternity did…freely, and unchangeably ordain whatsoever comes to pass: yet so, as thereby neither is God the author of sin, nor is violence offered to the will of the creatures." Godfrey's logic is akin to the adulterer saying, "God is sovereign over all things. So He is the One who has prevented me from being faithful to my wife." That sort of reasoning is unbecoming of someone with the theological prowess of Godfrey. But when it came to Covid-19, all bets were off.

Beyond the sheer falsity of Godfrey's theological claim, it fails on a more practical level. If God was the one who "stopped our worship as the gathered body of Christ on the Lord's Day" then why did many churches, unsurprisingly led by non-celebrity pastors, refuse to cancel the assembly of the saints? Did God prevent Godfrey's church and John MacArthur's church from gathering, but allowed Jon Speed's church to keep meeting? There is a *major* flaw in Godfrey's thinking.

There were many thoughtful Christians who, from the beginning, said that the church should never stop meeting. I was one of them, but I was prevented from meeting with the assembled church – not by God, but by my pastor and elders who immediately folded like a house of cards and ceased meeting for weeks on end. Similarly, the saints in Godfrey's church and MacArthur's church were prevented from assembling *not* by God, but by *Godfrey* and *MacArthur*, men who acted just like the world.[1]

It is worth reiterating that the churches that *never* cancelled in-person gatherings had the same information leaders such as Godfrey and MacArthur had. They had the same news media and government mandates. More importantly, they had the same church history books, and they had the same Bible. Bible-believers said the church must keep meeting long before we "knew the truth" about Covid-19. We said it right away.

Blaming God for the decisions of spineless

---

[1] I once heard the objection that maybe the senior pastor *wanted* to keep meeting with the sheep, but the elder board cancelled the assembly. I doubt that happened in any of the cases mentioned, but if it did, the pastor should have *defied* the elder board and obeyed God rather than man. If the elders locked him out of the church, he should have met with the sheep elsewhere.

church leaders is shameful. Furthermore, it does not lead to growth. It does not lead to growth because it subverts the need for repentance. The prophet Jeremiah needed to remind the people that it was because of *their* sin that judgment had come: "Hast not *thou* procured this unto *thyself*, because *thou* hast forsaken the Lord thy God?" (Jeremiah 2:17; cf. 4:18). They needed to understand that they had sinned. It did no good for them to look back with ignorance. It did no good for them to be oblivious like Malachi's priests. If pastors following Godfrey's example view the church closures as merely the result of God's will, then how will they learn to respond in the future? And, even more frightening, what will they tell God when he asks them how they led his sheep? Will they sound like Malachi's priests? "How did we scatter the sheep?" "How did we prevent the church from meeting?"

Even though I have learned much from some of their teachings, it behooves me to point out the errors of these "priests" and "shepherds," lest we find ourselves imitating the faithlessness and obliviousness of these men.

THE NARRATIVES WE SPIN

That John MacArthur is hailed as a courageous leader during the Covid-19 lockdown is utterly astounding and it is proof positive that the celebrity pastor model blinds the eyes and deafens the ears. MacArthur initially said it was an "easy call" to cancel church, and he, along with his fellow elders, officially cancelled the assembly of the saints for weeks on end. In a video posted on Grace Church's Facebook page on March 16, 2020, John MacArthur declared that the services were cancelled – but he also mentioned the "critical" need that church members keep giving money:

> Well, as you can tell, I'm sitting in an *empty worship center*. And that's the way it's gonna be, I think, for perhaps weeks, and maybe even into a *couple of months*. This is something unprecedented in my 51 years here – this has never happened before. But it is in the providence of God his purpose for us now…As we think about an empty auditorium we face a very real problem, and that is, this church is supported by the regular Sunday giving of all of you faithful members. *We're not going to be meeting for a while*, and that means we don't have the opportunity for that to be a part of our worship, so I just want to let you know that it's critical for us going forward…to make sure that we are still able to support the ministries that are ongoing here. *The services on Sunday are not happening*, the fellowship groups are not going on, but so many other ministries are flourishing. We're even making videos on a weekly basis to send out to families so they can have something to offer the children by way of Bible instruction.[2]

In the video, MacArthur went on to instruct people how to donate online via a "button on the website." He also explained that the church would send pre-

---

[2] Grace Community Church Facebook video, "An important message from our Pastor," 16 March 2020. Emphasis added.

paid envelopes to parishioners to allow them to send money to the church. The message was clear: The assembly of the saints is cancelled until further notice.

Over two months later, on May 22, 2020, MacArthur said the church would finally reopen. Following then-President Trump's announcement that churches were "essential," MacArthur said, "So in…response to the leadership of our president, we're gonna go to church. And we're going to go to church this Sunday [May 24, 2020]."[3] However, the next day, MacArthur backtracked:

> We were elated yesterday morning when President Trump declared churches to be essential, asked us to open this very Sunday, and promised to fight any state government that tried to stand in the way. As I've said many times, the Bible would have us submit to the governing authorities, and in the United States, there is no higher human executive authority than the president, who was speaking on a matter of federal and constitutional interest, specifically the First Amendment.
>
> With that said, at our last elder meeting, we talked about how this situation was changing not just day-by-day, but even hour-by-hour, and that sadly turned out to be true here. Late Friday night, the Ninth Circuit, which is generally known as the most left-wing and anti-biblical circuit court in the nation, ruled 2-1 in favor of California

[3] Transcript of a video by John MacArthur, retrieved from https://currentpub.com/2020/05/24/now-john-macarthurs-grace-community-church-will-not-open-tomorrow/

Governor Newsom's statewide stay-at-home order, rejecting an emergency motion to allow for religious services to proceed.[4]

MacArthur expressed his dissatisfaction with the court decision, but *consented* to follow it: "Even so, for now, the Ninth Circuit decision is sadly the law of the land in California, and we gladly submit to the sovereign purposes of God." He added:

> Separate and apart from the legal questions raised above, our worship services are not to be times of media circus and frenzy, particularly when we gather around the Lord's Table. To prevent that from occurring, the elders of Grace Community Church desire to delay our reopening and leave it in the hands of God…We will continue to meet with live stream at 10:30 AM and 6:00 PM, which obviously the Lord has blessed.

According to MacArthur's *own* words, the church was *still* not reopened by the end of May. In fact, a Facebook post from Grace Church dated May 23, 2020, stated the following: "Our campus reopening has been delayed. Read our statement: https://bit.l7/3ecklrO." The link to read the statement no longer functions, but it likely pointed

---

[4] From a statement from John MacArthur, retrieved from https://currentpub.com/2020/05/24/now-john-macarthurs-grace-community-church-will-not-open-tomorrow. The link to the statement (originally entitled "Ninth Circuit Court Rules Against the President and Churches") on Grace Church's website no longer works, but simply states: "We're sorry, the content you are looking for has expired."

back to the sections quoted above. The next day (May 24, 2020), a Facebook user named Lori Thornbrue commented on the post:

> I love the biblical wisdom of Pastor John, and have learned and listened to him for the 20 years since I became a believer. My question is this: Since we are instructed to congregate, since we are the body of Christ…at what point will Grace Community decide that it must defy a government that is diametrically opposed to Scripture? How many Sundays will need to go by?[5]

The same day, another user commented: "God said not to forsake the gathering of the saints. God's law trumps government's laws. I love your messages, but you guys should be open. Why are you putting the government above God?" Someone else wrote, "Saddened by this decision…I expected more from a (or so I thought) strong biblical leadership." In any case, despite calls for faithfulness, the clear message to the world was this: *Grace Church will remain closed.*

The next month, on June 24, 2020 (over *three months* after the mid-March shutdown of his church), a video was published on Grace Church's Facebook page. In that video, MacArthur admitted the church had *still not* fully opened:

> People keep asking me, "When are we going to have a full opening?" and I have no idea when that's going to come, because the ground is shifting underneath us as

---

[5] A comment on Grace Church's Facebook page. 24 May 2020.

you know. Every time we turn around there is a new kind of rule, and we are trying to find out who is really the authority, and what is a law, and who has the power to make a law…These are very difficult things to sort out…We're getting close to the point where we're going to have to decide whether we obey man or God, at the same time, we don't want to jeopardize anyone.[6]

So, *three months* after the initial shutdown MacArthur said the church is *now* "getting close" to having to decide if they will obey God or man.[7]

These comments from MacArthur are at odds with a statement published *over a year later* (in 2021) by the church. In that statement, the church declares that by "mid-May, large numbers of worshipers began returning on Sunday mornings spontaneously. The auditorium was well filled by early June."[8] And yet on June 24, 2020, MacArthur publicly announced to the world that the church had *not* yet fully opened, and they were *getting close* to deciding if they would obey man or God. It is possible that some parishioners *did* come back into the auditorium, but MacArthur's *official message* to the congregation (and the world) was that the church will continue to follow the mandates.

Finally, on July 31, 2020, over *four months after*

---

[6] Grace Community Church Facebook video, "A Mid-Week Message from Our Pastor - June 24, 2020."

[7] MacArthur's comments also reveal the consequences of an erroneous view of Romans 13. Namely, an inability to know who is "in charge." Is it the president? The court? The health department? A blithe submission to the state terminates in cluelessness.

[8] "Facing COVID-19 Without Fear," retrieved from www.gracechurch.org. Published 21 September 2021.

MacArthur and the elders suspended the assembly of the saints, a video was released by Grace Church wherein MacArthur declared that the church will now obey God, not man. In that video MacArthur said, "We will obey God rather than men."

> We're gonna be faithful to the Lord and we're gonna leave the results to him...We will not bow to Caesar...And that means that we will continue to gather as a church every Sunday. Every Sunday. That is not going to stop...We will be here; we will meet as the church of Jesus Christ because we're commanded to do that.[9]

The following chart summarizes the development in MacArthur's public statements:

May 23, 2020	June 24, 2020	July 31, 2020
"[F]or now, the Ninth Circuit decision is sadly the law of the land in California, and we gladly submit to the sovereign purposes of God."	"These are very difficult things to sort out...We're getting close to the point where we're going to have to decide whether we obey man or God, at the same time, we don't want to jeopardize anyone."	"We will obey God rather than men... We will be here; we will meet as the church of Jesus Christ because we're commanded to do that."

[9] Grace Community Church Facebook video, "An Important Update From Our Pastor." 31 July 2020.

Conspicuously missing from any public video or statement from MacArthur is a message of heartfelt *repentance*.

You will recall MacArthur's earlier words (from April 2020): "The clear demand of Scripture is to be subject to the [civil government]…We conform, we are submissive to the government…That was an easy call for us." An easy call? Failing to do what God commands was an easy call? But now many people think MacArthur stood as a bold example of faithfulness during Covid-19. The reason is that a narrative has been spun to make it appear that way. In May 2022, Grace to You hosted the (somewhat ironically named) *Truth Matters Conference* in Williamstown, Kentucky. During the Question-and-Answer panel discussions, MacArthur was presented as an example of bold faithfulness. And MacArthur readily accepted the approbation, saying:

> At Grace Church, we understood that Covid, and all that stuff, really provide an opportunity for hostile people to shut down the church. I don't think for a minute that we weren't an absolute target along with every other faithful church to be shut down. Well, we refused to do that because we are the church and the more danger there is in the world the more we need to be the church. So, we saw it as an assault, really, covertly, to take down faithful churches…If 10% of the people died, we'd have still been the church and done exactly what we did. Because that's why we're in the world and the more desperate times become the more faithful we need to be…The

church needs a massive dose of biblical fidelity and the courage of conviction to be the church.[10]

How MacArthur can publicly spin that narrative of "courage" and "conviction" without publicly repenting and apologizing for immediately shutting down his church, and not officially reopening until the end of July, is puzzling.

Furthermore, MacArthur's statement of *"I don't think for a minute that we weren't an absolute target along with every other faithful church to be shut down"* is clean contrary to what he said when he made the "easy call" to cancel church and blatantly stated that it was not a matter of persecution. When he initially shut down his church, he said this:

> What would have made a difference would have been if this was persecution of the church. If, all of the sudden, the government decided to shut down churches as an act of persecution against churches, we would defy that.[11]

That provides a nice copout.

Most strikingly, his comment that "if 10% of the people died, we'd have still been the church and done exactly what we did" is demonstrably untrue. After a long time trying "to find out who is really the authority," MacArthur finally officially opened the church. What changed his mind? Was it heartfelt

---

[10] John MacArthur, during a question-and-answer panel in May 2022.
[11] Grace to You, "Thinking Biblically About the COVID-19 Pandemic: An Interview with John MacArthur." Retrieved from YouTube.

repentance? *No*. Was it a recognition that he was wrong to ever cancel the assembly of the saints? *Nope*. Was it a willingness to be faithful, even "if 10% of the people died"? *Negative*.

In a 2021 statement released on Grace Church's website by MacArthur and the pastoral staff, he said the following:

> Since the true gravity of the threat was still unknown and the quarantine was supposed to be reasonably short, Grace Church's elders decided to suspend public services while we continued live-streaming sermons from the pulpit in the Worship Center auditorium…*More than six weeks* passed with no letup on the government-ordered quarantine. While media reports and health department predictions continued to be dire, the actual impact of the virus on our congregation was only mildly worse than the annual flu. Relatively few congregants tested positive, and those who did typically recovered quickly. It was soon obvious (and CDC statistics proved it) that healthy people in their fifties or younger were not in imminent mortal danger from the spread of COVID-19.[12]

Let's have some integrity and truthfulness here: MacArthur was *not* willing to be faithful even if it meant the death of "10% of the people" as he boldly claimed at the 2022 conference. He only opened the church when he realized Covid-19 was little more

---

[12] "Facing COVID-19 Without Fear," retrieved from www.gracechurch.org. Published 21 September 2021. Emphasis added.

than a bad flu. After sheltering in place for weeks like the pagans during the plague, Grace Church officially opened its doors. Long after faithful churches had been meeting for weeks (never having shut down), Grace Church finally decided to obey God. At *that* point, the church did face some opposition from the civil government, but their "stand" against the government at that point is not overly commendable – they were simply doing their duty, as all faithful churches *had already been doing*, while Grace Church's doors had remained officially closed. What would have been somewhat respectable, following the show of cowardice, would have been heartfelt *repentance* and an open admission that they should *never* have closed the church. That did not come. Instead, a narrative of courage and faithfulness was spun.

Perhaps this is because it's hard for celebrity pastors to repent. "It's hard for prominent Christian leaders to repent," MacArthur said at the *same* conference, when speaking about critical race theory. He then shared how he once preached a sermon on repentance:

> I asked the congregation, "How many of you have ever heard a pastor get up in his church and repent?" I didn't find anybody who said yes. Self-preservation plays a big role – and the lack of integrity at that point.[13]

In the words of the theologian Michael Jackson, MacArthur ought to start with "the man in the

---

[13] John MacArthur, during a question-and-answer panel in May 2022.

mirror." In the abovementioned 2021 church statement, MacArthur also lamented the confused state of many Christians:

> Oddly, some of the same evangelical leaders who insisted the church must shut down on orders from the state also published essays affirming the duty and priority of congregational worship. No wonder churchgoers are confused.[14]

As Nathan told David, "*You* are the man," John MacArthur!

MacArthur also wrote the following in 2021, "There is no justification for quarantining healthy people, and certainly no warrant for having the entire church suspend congregational worship on a prolonged basis." Upon hearing these statements, one has to wonder if MacArthur reads his own words. His 2021 statement closes with a rousing call to faithfulness:

> Now is not the time to forsake our own assembling together. The church must be the church – a pillar and buttress for the truth. We cannot cower in fear. We cannot hide our light under a bushel. We are not called to feed the fears of a world that is perishing.

So inspiring. There's only one problem. MacArthur didn't do any of those things. The churches that

---

[14] "Facing COVID-19 Without Fear," retrieved from www.gracechurch.org. Published 21 September 2021.

didn't shut down for those weeks and weeks while Grace Church was closed were the faithful ones. They did not cower in fear. Grace Church did.

In a sister statement by Grace Church's elders, entitled "Christ, not Caesar, Is Head of the Church," a compelling case is made that the state has no authority to tell the church what to do. Tucked away in the addendum of this statement, is an explanation (read: excuse) as to why Grace Church *still* shut down.

> The elders of Grace Church considered and independently consented to the original government order, not because we believed the state has a right to tell churches when, whether, or how to worship. To be clear, we believe that the original orders were just as much an illegitimate intrusion of state authority into ecclesiastical matters as we believe it is now. However, because we could not possibly have known the true severity of the virus, and because we care about people as our Lord did, we believe guarding public health against serious contagions is a rightful function of Christians as well as civil government. Therefore, we voluntarily followed the initial recommendations of our government. It is, of course, legitimate for Christians to abstain from the assembly of saints temporarily in the face of illness or an imminent threat to public health.

That is some revisionist history occurring before our very eyes. Remember what MacArthur said initially? "The clear demand of Scripture is to be subject to the [civil government]...We conform, we are submissive to the government…That was an easy call for us." Also recall his statement at the end of May 2020: "[F]or now, the Ninth Circuit decision is sadly the law of the land in California, and we gladly submit to the sovereign purposes of God." But now we are supposed to believe he and the elders rejected the government's authority over the assembly from the beginning?

Even if Covid-19 was as deadly as government media puppets claimed it was, the church should have *kept meeting.* To cancel the assembly of the saints out of fear of a sickness, and then to reopen upon realizing the threat was not that serious, is not commendable. It is cowardly.

In summary, Grace Church shut down right away, deemed an "easy call" by MacArthur. They only opened when they realized the Covid-19 virus was not dangerous – *not* because they were bold in the face of danger, but because it was nothing more than a bad flu. And MacArthur is hailed as a leader worthy of imitation? We have very low standards. If Covid-19 was a bit more serious, then it would have been fine to keep the doors shut until…when?

Contrary to MacArthur's grandiose claims, the evidence points clearly to the fact that Grace Church would *not* have "done exactly what [they] did" if 10% of the people died. The very reason they gave for reopening was that the threat of sickness was *low.* At the *same* 2022 conference where he said he would have opened if 10% of the people died, MacArthur affirmed this:

> Our initial reaction was, "Well, we don't want to kill anybody, so, okay, we'll do livestream"…A few weeks went by, and it became apparent to me…that they were lying about the death threat. And when we began to see…the statistics were somewhere around 99% survival, we knew we weren't going to kill people.[15]

So, his claim that they would have been faithful no matter the cost ("10%") is demonstrably contradicted by his *own* words, at the very *same* conference.

At that conference, Phil Johnson heaped praise on MacArthur, saying that he thinks that when MacArthur's biography is written "a major chapter in that book will chronicle your leadership at Grace Church during the Covid crisis." But why should MacArthur even be commended? He simply *started* doing his duty, officially opening in July 2020 – *without* repenting of his sin for shutting down the church. His example is not praiseworthy. The fact that it is celebrated reveals the shallowness of the evangelical church in America. That MacArthur and his church now have the audacity to profess to stand on the biblical truth that God commands the church to meet is *unbelievable*. That they can seriously claim to believe this when they shut their doors for *months* due to threats (from a virus or otherwise) defies belief.

HIDING FROM THE TRUTH

It has been suggested that pointing out the truth of what happened concerning MacArthur (or any other

[15] John MacArthur, during a question-and-answer panel in May 2022.

pastor who scattered the sheep) is not helpful for the church. Some claim that Christians do not need to know what really happened – we only need to be encouraged to stand against tyrannical government. I recently posted some quotes from MacArthur (highlighting his submission to the government in closing church) in response to one pastor's social media post about the *Essential Church* documentary. My post was deleted by the pastor, and I received this message: "Hey Chris, I'm deleting your post because I think it's unhelpful in energizing the church to stand against the tyrannical government. It's just in-house bickering." That response demonstrates one of the reasons I wrote this book. The pastor was not concerned with the *truthfulness* of the quotes, but merely with pragmatic efforts to "energize" the church.

As Christians, we are supposed to be about the *truth*. Tyrannical government is a problem, but cowardly pastors who will not repent of scattering the sheep is a *bigger* problem. And now, I am coming to be convinced that pastors who want to *hide* the truth are also more dangerous to the church than any government tyrant will ever be. By and large, the pastors are unwilling to humble themselves and repent of their sin – and MacArthur stands as the consummate example of that.

It does not serve the church to sweep the truth under the rug – doing so will not serve the interests of the true church of Jesus Christ. The stance of the pastor who deleted my post is essentially this:

"Speaking the truth is unhelpful in energizing the church to stand against the tyrannical government." That is wrong. We ought to heed the words of the Apostle Paul and "cast off lying, and speak every man *truth* unto his neighbor" (Ephesians 4:25).

I have lost nearly all respect for the Godfrey's and the MacArthur's, as well as those who provide cover for them. I do believe in repentance, however. And if they acknowledge their wrongdoing, we could at least begin to appreciate their example. Until then, they offer us nothing more than a shallow, insipid faith that reacts just like the world when things get difficult or dangerous. Worse still, the actions of these Christian leaders are whitewashed by followers who seem to care more about honoring a man than about the truth.[16] We ought to imitate the men who stand on God's Word no matter the cost, not those who twist Reformed doctrines or wait until it is "safe" to defy Caesar.

THEOLOGICAL GYMNASTICS

During the third century plague mentioned at the beginning of Chapter 2, the early Christians demonstrated that there was something more important than avoiding sickness – namely, showing love and mercy to others. Author Alvin J. Schmidt wrote about the contrast between the Christians and the pagans during the plague:

---

[16] Such whitewashing also reveals a recurring theme: an awareness by pastors who scattered the sheep that what they did was *wrong*, and a subsequent desire to suppress aspects of what happened.

Because eternal life awaited all those who believed and died in Christ, life on earth was not the ultimate value. Even if one died while caring for the sick, a greater and better life lay ahead; moreover, if a sick or dying person came to see and accept Christ's forgiveness, another soul was gained for eternal life.[17]

This mentality was absent among many pastors in 2020. The value and importance of shepherds meeting with their sheep was relegated to a non-essential function. If eternal life and spiritual health are not highly valued, it will be easy to cancel the assembly of the saints. In our final analysis of a church's excuse for scattering the sheep we will consider the rationale of Chris Walker, Senior Pastor of Westminster Presbyterian Church in Pennsylvania.

Walker claimed that there were "three clear biblical commands" guiding the church's decision to turn away the sheep from gathering for worship. In his own words:

1. First, God's word urges us to do all in our power for the protection and preservation of life.

2. The second biblical command for not meeting for worship is the call to love our neighbor.

3. Finally, Scripture urges us with surprising strength and clarity to obey our governing authorities.[18]

---

[17] Alvin J. Schmidt, *How Christianity Changed the World*, p. 153.
[18] The following quotes from Chris Walker were taken from a letter to the

Let's examine each of these excuses for scattering the sheep.[19]

1. The Protection and Preservation of Life
One section will suffice to demonstrate Walker's rationale concerning the "protection and preservation" of life:

> Jesus also addresses the tension between saving life and following Sabbath commands. He argues that if your son, or even your ox, falls into a well on the Sabbath, we would "work" to get him out and rescue him (Lk 14:5). Jesus also appeals to the example of David, who ate the holy bread which was unlawful to eat when he and his men were in need and had no food (Mk 2:25-27). While Jesus was directly addressing the Pharisees' mis-application of the Sabbath, his examples make it clear that the normal prohibitions and patterns may be temporarily suspended when life is on the line. As Jesus asked the Pharisees, "Is it lawful on the Sabbath to do good or to do harm, to save life or to kill?" (Mk. 3:4)

The logic is this: If gathering with the saints presents the possibility of danger to life, then the elders are authorized to tell all the sheep to stay away from their pastor and one another. We have already addressed

---

Westminster Congregation.

[19] Prior to publication, I reached out to Dr. Walker to inform him that his statements would be published and analyzed. I also invited him to join me for an in-person, recorded podcast discussion. He declined the invitation for a public interaction, but we did meet privately. I am thankful for his gracious interaction during that meeting.

this at length in Chapter 1, so only a few comments will be made here.

Does this fit with the message of the Bible and church history? *Certainly not.* Stephen was stoned to death because of his Christian witness, and yet the early Christians continued to meet and publicly proclaim Christ. Risks notwithstanding, pastors simply do not have the authority to tell their sheep to stay away from their shepherds "for their own safety." For example, in a Communist regime, an imprisoned pastor does not have the pastoral authority to forbid his sheep from visiting him in prison (in fulfillment of Hebrews 13:3). Such prison visitations could carry with them *serious risk* to the visiting Christian – he could be liable to be locked up as well (or murdered). If a parishioner died in the course of his risky visitation, the pastor would not have "blood on his hands" if he had not made a public statement forbidding people from visiting him in prison.

The pastor's job is *not* to protect his sheep from the possibility of physical harm. If that were the case, the surfer should face excommunication for his daring adventures in shark infested waters. So too should the Chinese Christian smuggling Bibles into North Korea. The pastor's job is to protect his sheep from spiritual harm – "And fear ye not them which kill the body, but are not able to kill the soul: but rather fear him, which is able to destroy both soul and body in hell" (Matthew 10:28). Yes, if an armed terrorist enters the assembly, the pastor should be willing to lay down his life in that case (after first *firing back* at the assailant),[20] but the idea of micro-managing the physical location of congregants is untenable. Despite Walker's best attempts at eisegesis, Jesus' comments about doing work on the Sabbath or eating the showbread have nothing to do with a pastor's duty to meet with his sheep.[21]

Excursus: Blizzards, Hurricanes, and Extreme Weather
What if a hurricane is barreling down on the church building – should the church still meet there? Wouldn't a concern for the protection of life cause the pastor to cancel the assembly of the saints? Let's address this topic (as Walker brings it up later in his list of excuses). Acts of nature are often posited as legitimate reasons to cancel the assembly of the saints. If the church should be closed for *these things*, then it follows that it could be closed indefinitely for a virus. This reasoning is faulty and built on a poor foundation. Extreme weather does *not* authorize a pastor to turn away his sheep. At the very least, the pastor might have to receive his sheep somewhere else – after all, we all must be *somewhere* on any given day, even during a snowstorm or a hurricane.

---

[20] See Charl Van Wyk's book, *Shooting Back: The Right and Duty of Self-Defence.*
[21] In this section, Walker also cites Leviticus 13 as justification for telling the sheep they could not gather with the shepherd. However, Leviticus 13 deals with a sick person *with* symptoms, not a healthy person without symptoms. Ernest Springer, in *Coronavirus and the Leadership of the Christian Church*, writes: "Certainly, if one is known to be sick…that could relate somewhat to the leprosy [law], and that person should remain apart until well again. However, *the laws of the Old Testament did not require the closing of God's house*, and therein lies the rub. *You do not quarantine the healthy, only the sick*. But church leadership effectively threw away the baby with the bath water" (p. 34-35, emphasis in original).

Let me begin by acknowledging that a storm might prevent a *pastor* from *arriving* at one geographical location, but it might *not* prevent some of his sheep from gathering *to him*. The pastor must be *somewhere* every Lord's Day. Wherever he is, he should not turn away the sheep that want to gather with him. In other words, if the sheep decide to stay home, *so be it* – but the shepherd is *not* authorized to tell them that they must *stay put*.

The concept of the parsonage might be helpful here. The parsonage (the pastor's residence) was generally situated very close to the church building, if not annexed to it. The idea was that the shepherd would always be available to gather with the sheep. In many ways, the issue of blizzards leading to the cancellation of the assembly of the saints is only a concern because we have abandoned the idea of the parsonage. In earlier times, and even in rural villages or small towns today, when nearly everyone lived within walking distance of the church, cancelling service for a snowstorm wouldn't even be considered. If someone cannot make it to the assembly, then the pastor can perhaps provide visitation after the service or later in the week. What I am saying is this: At the *very least* a pastor should be willing to receive his sheep *where he is*. If his sheep come to him on the Lord's Day (and he ought to tell them they are *welcome* to come to him!) then he should receive them.[22] It is his duty.

---

[22] This is an indirect argument against megachurches, especially ones with *multiple* services. The assembly is meant to assemble as *one* group, in *one* place. However, even a large church, forced out of its meeting place, should find a farmer's field or a Solomon's Portico to meet in. Christians

Churches should plan for alternatives to cancelling the assembly of the saints during extreme weather. Many congregants may choose to shelter in place (especially if they live very far from the place of meeting), but others might not. If my brother came to my home during a hurricane or snowstorm, I would not turn him away and say, "You should not have come here and risked your life to spend the day with me. I cannot receive you." I would welcome him. The pastor should do the same. We are exhorted, "Be not forgetful to entertain strangers" (Hebrews 13:2). How much *more* should the pastor be willing to meet with his *own* sheep? If the pastor's residence is not within walking distance to the church meeting place, other contingency plans should be put in place. For example, to return to Walker's case, Westminster Presbyterian Church had approximately *eight* pastors and *fourteen* elders in 2020.[23] Not *one* of those men was willing to assemble with the saints during Covid-19? Not *one* of those men was willing to read the Bible, pray, sing a psalm, and exhort the sheep that were willing to gather on the Lord's Day? Not a single *one* of them? It appears not. What then, I ask, is their use?

2. Love of Neighbor

Showing "love" to neighbor was heralded as the great justifier of cancelling church for many pastors, including Walker. He wrote:

---

in the past have made do with less.
[23] This is based on staff listings in 2023.

While we should not dishonor God in order to be considerate to another, these verses make it clear that spurning our neighbor's life and well-being is also dishonoring to God unless there is a clear biblical mandate to ignore their good. The need to temporarily suspend meeting in order love each other and our neighbor during this pandemic has been evident from examples we have seen in South Korea and in France, where churches were the center of large community outbreaks. Gathering for worship in these situations not only led to deaths in the church, but in their communities as well. Meeting in the face of spreading death smacks more of arrogance than love for God and our neighbor.

Once again, granting the months-long gullibility of pastors like Walker who fell for the Covid-19 narrative of "mass outbreaks," the church *still* should have remained open. The verbal gymnastics, however, are impressive. Meeting with your spiritual family is "spurning our neighbor's life"? According to that logic, when I had dinner night after night with my family during Covid-19, I was spurning their lives. Or how about when several families voluntarily assembled, week after week, at my home for meals and fellowship in early 2020 – no masks, no distancing? Were we all partaking in some sort of kamikaze pact? Walker's words have not aged well. In fact, as mentioned previously, even Walker himself would be guilty of "spurning" his neighbor's life by his actions of meeting one-on-one with many different Christians, some elderly, and thus risking the further spread of a "deadly" virus.

Walker wrote that "[m]eeting in the face of spreading death smacks more of arrogance than love for God and our neighbor." Arrogance? Walker needs to explain how it is arrogant for Christians to desire fellowship during *any* health or national crisis. Once again, the pastoral-nanny mentality is evident here: These people are not wise enough to decide if they are vulnerable or not – nor are they able to make value judgments about the importance of human interaction, even during a "crisis" – we will make the decision for them. That sounds more akin to arrogance than choosing to meet with one's spiritual family.

3. Obey the Government

Walker's final justification for turning away the sheep focused on government recommendations.

> The Westminster Confession also argues that it is the duty of the civil magistrate "to take order, that unity and peace be preserved in the Church" (WCF 23.3). In Pennsylvania, our governor has acted with that goal. He has not made it illegal for churches to meet and has left it to churches to act with discretion. But he has pleaded with and counselled them not to meet for their safety and the safety of our communities around them, just as he has with all large gatherings. Since the government's role and focus is on physical safety while the church focuses on spiritual priorities, it may well be that Westminster will decide to meet again before the

government recommends that we do so. But only a strong case that the spiritual risks of not meeting now outweigh the physical risks of meeting should override the counsel given by God-given authorities for the safety of our congregation and community.

Beyond the ridiculous claim that Pennsylvania Governor Tom Wolf (an abortion-supporting, sodomy-approving enemy of Christ) was acting to preserve unity and peace in the Church is the telling admission that the civil government in Pennsylvania did *not* even force the churches to shut down. As my Pastor Joel Saint has said, Joseph Stalin, who had to resort to strong-arm tactics to shut down Christian churches, should have tried the Covid-19 approach: just ask the pastors to stop meeting.

Despite the admission that the civil government left it to the "discretion" of the churches in Pennsylvania, Walker *still* relied heavily on his supposed duty to "submit" to the civil government when asked to cancel church. As addressed in the foreword of this book, a twisting of Romans 13 was commonplace among pastors in 2020. Romans 13 clearly teaches that the civil government's role is to punish *evildoers*, not dictate when people can assemble as the body of Christ. The mindset of pastors like Walker often terminates in a nearly universal call for submission to the civil government, no matter what they demand. At best, these pastors might reserve a small place for civil disobedience if the government calls on Christians to physically bow down to an idol, but other areas of Christian obedience (assembling with the saints, getting married, educating children, etc.) are subservient to what the government demands (or, in the case of Pennsylvania in 2020, what the government recommends). Would Walker be consistent and send his children to a government school if the state mandated it? *Recommended* it?

Appeals to an unbiblical notion of blithe submission to the civil government notwithstanding, in Walker's case the government of Pennsylvania only *recommended* the churches close. In the end, for Walker, the decision to meet with believers became a risk analysis operation. Walker wrote:

> In many ways, we follow these principles every year when we cancel church for a snowstorm or choose individually to stay home from church due to illness. What is unique during this present time is that our time away from church has been longer.

I have addressed above why we should not "cancel" church, even for a snowstorm. Walker assumes such a practice is legitimate when it is not. But then he conflates that situation with an *individual* not attending the assembly due to an illness. Neither of those situations has any bearing on whether the elders of the church are authorized to tell *all* the sheep to stay home. Walker's logic, like Godfrey's and MacArthur's, is flawed to the point of ludicrousness; but attempts at justifying unbiblical actions inevitably terminate in illogical and ludicrous excuses. Pastors, of all people, should know this – how many of them have heard excuses for sin while counseling others?

Keep things simple men: *The pastor is always willing to meet with the sheep*. If these men are afraid of legal liabilities, they can have the congregants sign a waiver disclaiming the pastor from all responsibility for the individual choices of his sheep. Maybe that sort of safety net is what these men need to act boldly.

ATTEMPT TO SAVE FACE

Following his three excuses for cancelling church, Walker does an about-face and tries to argue that the assembly of the saints is commanded,[24] and we ought to meet *even if* danger exists. He prefaces that argument with these words:

> The above arguments for not meeting for worship are not meant to indicate that any level of risk should lead to the cancellation of worship. Westminster's pastors and elders are equally concerned that we not be overly cautious and unbiblically prevent God's people from gathering for worship.

However, because Walker and his elders had already *prevented* the people of God from gathering for worship, they had *already* acted unbiblically. They were in the company of Pharoah (cf. Exodus 9:1).

---

[24] Walker wrote: "Scripture makes it clear that gathering together for worship is the *commanded* pattern for God's people...This is why the Westminster Confession states that *public* and private exercises of worship on Sunday are a 'positive, moral, and perpetual *commandment*' (WCF 21.7)." Emphasis added.

Nevertheless, Walker had the audacity to claim that Westminster Presbyterian Church could serve as a beacon of strong moral vision and hope, despite the fact that they shut down like the rest of the world due to the fear of death:

> In addition, while gathering together presents some amount of risk to our community, we also believe that the church's moral vision, solid peace before a sovereign God, and message of hope in Christ are exactly what our community needs in the face of a pandemic.

Walker also wrote:

> So, in the face of fear, it is precisely meeting together as soon as it is not rash to do so that recognizes that this present world is passing away, but our hope is focused on another that is yet to come.

Walker's selective obedience jumps off the page. When *he and his elders* are willing to "risk it," *then* the assembly of the saints is what the community needs. (So, if a parishioner dies *at that point*, then his hands are clean?) The church elders will stand boldly in the face of fear once it is not *rash* to do so. That provides a nice escape hatch: Whenever it is dangerous to be faithful, then faithfulness is rash; when it is safe to be faithful, then we will stand in the "face of fear."

Meanwhile, some members of Walker's church had been pleading with their leaders to act like men from the beginning. Their pleas went unheeded by

Walker and the elders. When Westminster Presbyterian Church finally did reopen, the elders initially required face masks for admission to the Lord's Supper. One parishioner in Walker's church wrote the following in his personal journal[25] on June 13, 2020, concerning that decision:

> Having been raised in a Christian setting, I have heard the term "fencing the Lord's table" in various denominational contexts most of my life. This has always rightly and biblically referred to not allowing unbelievers to participate in this sacrament, thereby bringing damnation on the person participating unworthily (I Cor. 11:17ff). In a dramatic irony, tomorrow [my wife] and I are fenced out of the Lord's table for the first time in our collective 75 ½ years of active participation in church membership. Why? Because we refuse to participate in a service of masked pretenders.
>
> Our church...where we have been members since November 2014 – has a policy (5/13/20) in place which states: "Most importantly, [leadership] expects all attenders to wear a mask or face shield while on church property. If you are unwilling to wear a mask, we ask that you continue worshipping through the live stream at home." In a six-page response (5/20/20) to our [leadership], we have critiqued their policy both medically and theologically. We ended our response by excusing ourselves from church attendance while these restrictions are in place "because integrity does not

---

[25] The entry was shared later via public e-mail newsletter.

permit us to accommodate illusion." Despite medical, historical, confessional, and ecclesiastical challenges to [leadership's] guidelines from us and others, these have fallen largely on deaf ears. Or, as a physician friend from another state has said, "[Leadership] has lost its way."

Sometime back, our church had rightly explained why we do not believe in participating in virtual communion. Ironically, I suppose for the "non-elect" who either refuse to attend or who are outside the 250-number cap on service attendance, virtual communion will do just fine.

I thought I'd click on the link to sign up for service, just to see what happens. It took me out to Eventbrite (I thought I must be purchasing tickets for the Star Barn.) On that site, it stated: "Please do not come if you have COVID-19 symptoms [reasonable] and please let us know if you or a household member develop symptoms or receive a positive diagnosis within 14 days of your attendance since this means you could have unknowingly been infectious." It appears the Nanny church is alive and well. Suddenly, the church's modus operandi has become – "your health and safety are our top priority." Almost Gestapo-like, I suppose unmasked attenders would be met at the door with a mask-carrying [leadership] member in the true spirit of "violators will be prosecuted." Ironically, the church has now added both public health and law enforcement to their ecclesiastical duties.

Despite the fact that this (coronavirus and how to deal with it) is something that professionally we know a good bit about, that doesn't seem to matter. I could review the 13 Covid-positive patient records from the past week or two in our practice, but that doesn't seem to matter either. Never mind that they're all doing just fine. We pray daily that God preserves our witness and that we would be spared a spirit of bitterness. But a trust has been broken, and I fear it will be very difficult if not impossible to restore. God help us all.

That parishioner, at least for a time, left the church.[26] As he wrote, trust had been broken.

I would like to reiterate that if any of these man (MacArthur, Walker, etc.) would openly repent and admit their failure and cowardice, things could *begin* to move in the right direction. I am not a model of boldness and strength, but if my fear of death prevented me from protecting my wife or children, I hope I would at least be willing to publicly repent of my cowardice and resolve to never fail in such a shameful manner again. Can you imagine if Peter never repented of his denial of Christ? If Peter had remained obstinate, he would not have been restored, and he would not have boldly preached on the Day of Pentecost. I wonder what opportunities have been missed by men like MacArthur and Walker who have refused to humble themselves and own their failure? These pastors, and thousands more, refuse to humble themselves. Instead, they continue to offer excuses.

---

[26] He apparently returned later.

4

THE BLIND GUIDES

Perhaps I should have opened a book like this with the following query: *Is it ever proper to publicly correct the religious leaders of the day?*

Was such a practice only proper in the first century – when Jesus and John the Baptist called into question the faithfulness of the religious leaders of their day? Or is there ever a time for us to say that the professing evangelical and Reformed church is out of step with Scripture? Is it ever proper to hold up the practices of the religious leaders of our day to the Word of God?

If we say, "no," then we are saying that the professing evangelical and Reformed church can never stray, can never err.[1] We are saying that she can never be in danger of worldliness. If we cannot correct the professing church, then the church can

---

[1] At the very least, we are saying that no one can *call out* her leaders when she does. Or perhaps some will say that only a certain, select few (elder boards, presbyteries, etc.) can do so – but if said groups were doing their jobs in calling out the leaders of the church, then there would be no need for this book.

never be wrong. That sounds more like Roman Catholicism than biblical Christianity.

Some people will argue that in writing what I write, I am offending the leaders of the professing church. They will label a book like this as "in-fighting" or "uncharitable." I think they are quite wrong. Judgment begins with the house of God. If Christians cannot police themselves or clean house, then we are in no position to call a watching world to repent. Seeking to maintain some sort of "quasi-unity" in order to put forth the *appearance* that the church is united is not what biblical unity is.

Others will say this is a private matter that should be dealt with behind closed doors. I disagree. We are talking about the professing evangelical and Reformed church and her *leaders*. The messages they sent and the practices they encouraged have been spread to the world.[2] It behooves all Christians to tell a watching world that so much of what they saw was not in step with the Bible. Frankly, I'm embarrassed by what I've seen from church leaders – cancelling services, telling congregants to stay six feet away from their brothers and sisters in Christ, requiring masks for the Lord's Supper, etc. And it's not simply that this was a moment of weakness – church leaders *consciously* made these decisions and then did not repent of them.

Also, consider the fact that Jesus openly critiqued

---

[2] And now, some (like Grace Church via a feature length documentary) are broadcasting to the world that they were examples of boldness during Covid-19.

the respected religious leaders of his day. And it is not as if Jesus was the only one who critiqued the Pharisees. Some will say, "Well, Jesus critiqued the Pharisees, but he was the only one with authority to do that because he knew them perfectly; therefore, you do not have authority to critique the religious leaders of our day." The problem with that is not only did Jesus criticize the religious leaders, but so also did John the Baptist. And not only did John the Baptist oppose them, but so too did the apostles when they refused to obey them and called into question their faithfulness to God (cf. Acts 4:19). Many Christians in 2020 had to not only disobey the government, but also their pastors in order to obey God and gather with their fellow believers.

When John the Baptist and Jesus critiqued the scribes and Pharisees, it is interesting that the main offense the religious leaders took was simply that they were being corrected. The religious leaders didn't really deal with the actual critiques: *The offense of John the Baptist and Jesus was mainly in the fact that they were critiquing the religious leaders.* One of my favorite lines comes from Luke 11 when one of the lawyers (a scholar of Torah) responds to Jesus' woes on the Pharisees. The lawyer answers Jesus, "Teacher, in saying these things you insult us also" (Luke 11:45, ESV). The lawyer sort of says: "Hey, you seem to be implying that we could be sinning too." What does Jesus say? Does he say, "Sorry, I didn't mean to include you in this statement. I am simply making a general statement; I don't mean to question your faithfulness"? No! He says, "Woe be to you also, ye Lawyers" (Luke 11:46).

What I have found is that when the professing church – and I am *not* talking here about liberal churches that have long ago abandoned the gospel – is critiqued by any number of voices from within her ranks, the response from church leaders is often something along the lines of, "You are suggesting that we are in sin," or, "You are saying that we didn't follow the Bible when we made our decision" – as if the accusation is *by default* unwarranted, or that it is unchristian to even suggest such a thing. The critique is often only addressed in a superficial manner, and the focus is rather on the fact that they were critiqued. I have seen this at the level of small local churches and at the larger level of critiques against the broader evangelical and Reformed church.

In 2020, many Christians called on the professing church and her leaders to repent of the sin of ceasing to meet in the name of Jesus, or of forcing congregants to bow to the state when it comes to assembling. Many of the responses by church leaders were along the lines of:

> *"Are saying that all these churches that stopped meeting sinned?"*

> *"Are you suggesting that they didn't put God's Word first?"*

> *"Are you are saying that they conformed to the world?"*

Yes, that is *exactly* what we are saying. Simply stating

that the critique implies that sin could be involved does not make it void. If the professing church cannot understand that she is susceptible to worldliness and sin – even apostasy – then she truly is blind, but it wouldn't be the first time that religious leaders were blind guides leading the blind.

These things ought not be so. The professing church and her leaders must never become so comfortable that they think they are immune to straying from the Bible in practice or doctrine. Part of the solution to this problem is for us to better understand the religious leaders of Jesus' day and how he viewed them. We often think of the Pharisees as a group who were viewed by the people as hypocritical leaders or false teachers. This was not the case. If we better understand how they were viewed and why Jesus critiqued them, we can form a better understanding of the dangers facing us today.

BLIND GUIDES

So, let's consider the "blind guides" of Jesus' day. By looking at Matthew 15 and Matthew 23, I will briefly point out four things about the religious leaders of Jesus' day. For each point I will make application to the religious leaders of our day.

1. They sat "on Moses' seat" – they taught the truth; they were orthodox, not liberal, in theology (Matt. 23:2).

Note, first of all, that the scribes and Pharisees were people whose teaching Jesus commended! He told his followers to do whatever they said (Matthew 23:2-3). You see, the scribes and Pharisees were not the religious liberals of the day. They were not viewed by faithful Jews as unqualified leaders. They were respected, honored, and revered – much like many of the Reformed authors, conference speakers, and church leaders who led the way in cancelling church.

The Pharisees were the religious conservatives who held to God's Word and sought to guide and protect the people from spiritual error. They were the graduates from the Reformed theology seminaries, if you will. The equivalent of the scribes and Pharisees today would *not* be a Rob Bell or a Bart Ehrman or a United Church leader proclaiming a false gospel. The closest corollary today would be the Reformed and evangelical leaders who have the gospel of grace correct, who rightly taught about the saints' duty to obey God in all things – those whom Jesus would say, "practice and observe whatever they tell you" (but not necessarily what they do)! I don't question the fact that the Reformed church leaders often teach right doctrine – they *previously* taught about the duty of the saints to assemble, no matter what.

It is not as if these churches didn't believe that God had commanded them to meet. John MacArthur, who immediately cancelled services, who said that it was an "easy call" to stop gathering, had previously written that, "collective and corporate worship [is] a vital part of spiritual life." And even while openly saying it was an "easy decision" to cancel church, he acknowledged that "God says we must meet." Again, this was the consistent teaching within the Reformed church. They *did* teach the correct doctrine. Years ago, long before Covid-19, R.C. Sproul taught about the command to gather together, even calling on wives to disobey the authority of their husbands if the husband forbade the wife from assembling with the saints:

> I don't know how many times I have women say to me, "I'm trying to be submissive to my husband, but my husband won't allow me to go to church. What should I do?" I said, "You go to church on Sunday morning. You disobey your husband. Because *God commands you not to forsake the assembling together of the saints.* And here is one case where not only may you disobey, but you must disobey. And then try to win [your husband] with your love and subjection the rest of the week."[3]

Sproul was being consistent with the Christian worldview. He was accurately applying the doctrine to life. He also said:

> If any ruler – a governing official or body, schoolteacher, boss, or military commander – commands you to do something God forbids or forbids you from doing something God commands, not only may you disobey, but you must disobey. If it comes down to a choice like this, you must obey God.[4]

---

[3] Exposit the Word. "Romans 13:1-3 'Submit to Government' Line by Line Bible Study with R.C. Sproul." Emphasis added.
[4] R.C. Sproul, *What Is the Relationship Between Church and State?*

Christians would have been wise to follow Jesus' advice regarding the religious leaders: *Practice what they say, but don't do what they do*. When the Covid-19 compromise occurred, Christians should have listened to the teaching of the Reformed church *prior* to the "outbreak."

For years, many Christians within the church have been calling for a more faithful conformity to what is taught by church leaders. The professing Reformed church proclaims that the gospel of grace is the only true gospel, and then takes it easy on false gospels. The professing church claims to be "together for the gospel," or united in a "gospel coalition," but then is not firm on the gospel when it comes to teaching it with clarity, precision, and discrimination against false doctrine. Another area of concern has been the Law of God. Reformed teachers give lip service to God's Law, but then shy away from applying God's Law to the civil sphere.[5] These are all signs of a disconnect between beliefs and practice. This disconnect became painfully obvious when the Reformed church at large cancelled church.

So, both the religious leaders of Jesus' day and the Reformed pastors of our day taught the correct thing, but then they didn't do it.

---

[5] For more on applying God's Law to the civil realm, see my book, *Seven Statist Sins: The Capital Vices of Civil Government in American Society*, and Luke Saint's book, *The Sound Doctrine of Theocracy*.

2. In practice, the religious leaders of Jesus' day placed other things (tradition, the teachings of man) above the Word of God (Matt. 15:4-9).

The Pharisees, the religious leaders of the day, claimed to hold to God's Word above all else. These would have been the ones hosting the conferences on Scripture and faithfulness to God. Yet they tended to place other things above Scripture. In Jesus' day it was tradition, things that men had said were important. Though ostensibly seeking to be faithful to God and his Word, they actually disregarded God's Word for the sake of their tradition (their man-made laws).

In Matthew 15, Jesus points out that they had a clear command from God: "Honor thy father and mother." The problem with the Pharisees here was that while they acknowledged that command from God, they turned around and encouraged the people to disobey it by introducing another standard: "But you say, 'Whoever says to his father or mother, "Whatever profit you might have received from me is a gift to God" – then he need not honor his father or mother.' Thus you have made the commandment of God of no effect by your tradition" (Matthew 15:5-6, NKJV). The majority of modern church leaders did the same thing in 2020. They loosely *acknowledged* the command from God – the church must meet – and then they prevented the people from obeying it by introducing some other standard – namely, a doctrine of man (whether from some council of pastors, or the CDC, or the governor's office).

God commands his people to gather together in fellowship. For centuries, Christians believed this, and even at great risk to themselves, even in opposition to government mandates, they chose to gather. Even church leaders that capitulated and stopped meeting *said* they believed this. Then, with the world watching in 2020, the professing evangelical and Reformed church – with the exception of a faithful remnant – capitulated and ceased meeting. They gave up on gathering together in the name of Jesus. They stopped coming together because of a concern for sickness, or a concern for a fine, or a concern to be viewed a certain way. Whatever the reason, they cancelled church. As the world watched, the professing church put fellowship and the clear direction from God's Word aside and elevated the *doctrines of men* instead.

3. They said they believed one thing, and then they did something else in practice – in other words, they were hypocrites (Matt. 23:27-28).

Jesus called the religious leaders of his day hypocrites. He didn't do this because they were charlatans or slick shysters. They were hypocrites because their practices did not conform with what they taught. Again, the Pharisees didn't come out and say they didn't believe in God's Word. They appeared righteous to others. They were ostensibly the best examples of faithfulness and orthodoxy of the day. When you think of the Pharisees, think of the group of religious leaders today that you most respect – think of the graduates of the Reformed seminaries. That's how the Pharisees were viewed, but they were hypocrites.[6] And many of the evangelical and Reformed leaders today are hypocrites. They don't practice what they preach.

Regarding the assembly of the saints, it was not as if the professing Reformed church had no idea what was at stake here. It was not as if they had never thought about the idea of authorities forbidding something God commands. And it was not as if they didn't believe that God commanded the saints to gather. They said they believed this, and then they acted differently. That is at least a form of hypocrisy, by any honest standard. Hypocrisy is defined as "the practice of claiming to have moral standards or beliefs to which one's own behavior does not conform."

If the immediate response from a church leader who cancelled services is, "Hey, are you accusing me of hypocrisy? How uncharitable and un-Christlike," then we have a problem. The professing church and her leaders are not open to correction and reform. The response of the professing evangelical and Reformed church reminds me very much of the scribes and Pharisees in the first century.

Even before the Covid-19 compromise, many of these churches claimed to be Reformed, claimed to have the gospel, but hid it under a lampstand. And

---

[6] At least most of them – and this is a justification for painting with a broad brush on occasion. Some Pharisees were genuine – just like some modern church leaders who did not cancel church. They stand as examples to the rest.

now, their true colors have come out even more clearly. The writing is on the wall: The professing evangelical and Reformed church is good at preaching doctrine, but bad at living it out. Just like the scribes and Pharisees, they know what to say, but they do not practice what they preach. And as such, the world sees a confusing display of Christianity.

4. They revered those who went before them in "church history," garnishing the tombs of the righteous, but did not follow in their footsteps (Matt. 23:29-31).

The Pharisees admired the prophets that had unflinchingly stood for faithfulness to God. The scribes respected those who would not capitulate to the world or undermine the Word of God, but it was all for show. Jesus said to them:

> Woe be unto you, Scribes and Pharisees, hypocrites: for ye build the tombs of the Prophets, and garnish the sepulchers of the righteous, And say, If we had been in the days of our fathers, we would not have been partners with them in the blood of the Prophets. So then ye be witnesses unto yourselves, that ye are the children of them that murdered the Prophets. Fulfill ye also the measure of your fathers. (Matthew 23:29-32)

The scribes and Pharisees were like those today who write the books about John Knox and William Bradford. They were like those today who talk about how the Reformers stood on the Word of God against the world. They were like those today who admired the first-century Christians or the 17th century Pilgrims for refusing to cancel church, even at great risk to themselves. They were like those people today, who say all those things, and then, when it comes to their own lives and their own day, when the rubber meets the road, when faithfulness will mean something, they abandon the way of righteousness and faithfulness. They are hypocrites, garnishing the tombs of the righteous, while simultaneously ostracizing their spiritual heirs.

WARNING FOR OUR DAY

There are uncanny similarities between the Pharisees and the leaders of the professing evangelical and Reformed church. Both groups taught the correct doctrine, both groups then strayed from that doctrine in practice, putting another standard higher than God's Word, and both groups said they admired those who went before them, only to do the exact opposite. These warnings were written for our instruction. The church leaders of our day would be wise to heed them. If the professing evangelical and Reformed church does not wake up and realize she has sinned, then we will continue to be led by blind guides.

I can understand and accept a Christian failing to honor Christ in a moment of weakness, if he or she is broken over that failure and desirous to honor Christ in the future, no matter the cost. I cannot accept a conscious decision to give up on doing what God requires because doing so will cost us something. That is not a religion I want to be part of and those are not religious leaders we should follow. The loving thing to do is to warn others about such blind guides.

If I wrote about the errors of Rob Bell, or the errors of liberal "church leaders" who have accepted the sin of homosexuality – if I wrote about *those* "church" leaders, no one within the professing Reformed church would raise an eyebrow. They've forgotten that when Jesus critiqued the Pharisees (which he did often!), he did not do so because it was widely accepted that these were the false teachers. Jesus spoke so much about the Pharisees because the people *did* respect them. He spoke so forcefully because not only were the *leaders* blind, but the *people* had been blinded too.

If we do not understand that the leaders within even the Reformed church can be blind guides, then we are in great danger of the same errors that plagued the people in Jesus' day. The Pharisees had enough to persuade the people to kill Jesus. The Reformed leaders of our day had enough influence to persuade a great many to neglect the assembly of the saints. These things ought not to be so. There is a place for religious leaders, but every Christian must take the Word of God and judge the teaching and *practices* of such leaders by that Word.

May the Lord be pleased to grant us a new reformation, in which he will raise up new leaders who will stand on his Word, who will practice what they preach, who will follow in the steps of faithful Christians from the past, and who will never again scatter the sheep. And may he be pleased to grant the rest of us eyes to see the truth – and the nous to know when to stop following the blind guides.

5

THE APOLOGY THAT NEVER CAME

In 1995, dc Talk released the song, "What If I Stumble?" The song starts with someone reading these lines:

> The greatest single cause of atheism in the world today is Christians who acknowledge Jesus with their lips, then walk out the door and deny Him by their lifestyle. That is what an unbelieving world simply finds unbelievable.

Like it or not, true Christians must deal with the consequences of the professing church. Sadly, many unbelievers look at the professing church's lack of faithfulness and conclude that such is what true Christianity is. As such, for many a true follower of Jesus, the response of the professing evangelical and Reformed church during Covid-19 has been one of the most discouraging and disheartening periods of the past century. Dealing with government overreach, media-induced fear, and hysteria without end would have been bad enough. But the one place where

Christians *should* have been able to find refuge was in the church. There, believers should have found a different spirit – a spirit of faith and trust and courage. A spirit of freedom and peace. Believers should have been able to point to the church – the called-out ones – and say to a watching world, "Behold, there is something otherworldly, something different." Sadly, that wasn't the case for most churches. Uncertainty, fear, cancellations of fellowship, mask requirements, and social distance regulations thrived in the church just as in the world.

What follows is what I believe the professing evangelical and Reformed church *should* say to America. And, of course, she should not only say it, but change course accordingly.

THE APOLOGY

America, we're sorry. We had a once-in-a-lifetime opportunity to show you how different Christianity is from the world, and we failed.

Years ago, Leonard Ravenhill said, "The world out there is not waiting for a new definition of Christianity; it's waiting for a new demonstration of Christianity." The Covid-19 debacle was the perfect opportunity for us to give you that new demonstration of Christianity. We could have shown you what it means to live a life free from fear. We could have shown you what it means to value spiritual things more than material things. We could have shown you that Christians are different. Instead, most evangelical churches acted just like the world. Our profession of faith made little difference in our lives. Our churches closed their doors just like the Lion's Club and the community BINGO night. It's too late for us now to change how we responded, and the least we can do is say that we're sorry.

We're sorry we contradicted so much of what we had told you previously. Prior to the coronavirus, we told you that it was vital for Christians to gather together and fellowship. We preached about passages such as Hebrews 10:25: "not forsaking the assembling of ourselves together, as is the manner of some, but exhorting one another, and so much the more as you see the Day approaching" (NKJV). We told you about Christians throughout church history who were willing to meet despite the dangers of persecution, oppression, and even death. We held these men and women up as examples of faithfulness. And then, when the coronavirus struck us, we scattered like so many cockroaches in the night. Worse, our shepherds scattered their own sheep. Forgive us.

Prior to the coronavirus we told you that living for Christ was worth more than anything this world could offer, including safety, health, and prosperity. We told you about Christians – going all the way back to the apostles – who truly understood the gospel and were willing to give up everything to follow Jesus. We told you about the missionaries and housewives, preachers and plowboys, who were willing to die if they could only read the Scripture. We told you that obedience to Christ was not an optional part of discipleship, but the very essence of following Jesus.

And then, when it was going to cost us something to stand for Jesus and stand against the world, we crumbled like a child's sandcastle under a tidal wave. Forgive us.

We're sorry we perverted the glorious and beautiful blessing of Christian fellowship. We neglected fellowship. For some of us, it didn't even take one week for us to cancel fellowship. We dressed it up with a lot of explanations and qualifications, but the bottom line is that we told everyone to stop meeting together as a church body. We did not accurately demonstrate the doctrine of Christian fellowship. We made Christianity to look no different than a social club or sports league, willing to cancel gatherings on the word of a pagan tyrant or the threat of a sickness.

But even worse than abandoning Christian fellowship, we perverted fellowship. We encouraged you to think that Christians view "online" events as gatherings, fellowship, or services. This is all a gross perversion of what God intended for the church. We know that none of these things are fellowship, but we continued to act as if they were. To our shame, when we finally found some courage to meet, we continued to enforce mask and distancing mandates. We showed that we really don't care if true fellowship occurs – where believers can interact with one another, see each other's faces, and act as family – we only cared about continuing to present a façade of Christianity. We did have good motives and intentions, but the road to hell is paved with good intentions. Truth be told, we caved to the pressure. Our actions are a stain upon the true church's testimony concerning the doctrine of Christian fellowship.

We're sorry we conformed to the world. Christians are supposed to look different from the world. The fear that characterizes so much of our world, amplified to the extreme during the coronavirus, is unbecoming of a true Christian church. We know that we have been charged to not be conformed to this world (or "age," see Romans 12:2). However, we found the temptation too strong and the potential cost too high for us to have our minds transformed during the coronavirus. Instead of standing as a city upon a hill, as a light for a lost world, we acted just like everyone else. Just like the pagans in the plagues of the second and third centuries, we encouraged you to stay away from others.

We understand if you now view Christianity as simply a pie-in-the-sky religion that has no real practical consequences for life. We lived as if that was the case. You might not believe us now – and we can hardly blame you based on how we have responded – but that's not true Christianity. Please overlook our horrible example.

We're sorry we made our faithful brothers and sisters – those churches that stood firm from the very *beginning* of the Covid-19 lockdowns – look like outliers and pariahs. While most of the professing church conformed to the world's thinking, a faithful remnant of congregations did not soil their garments with the fear and paranoia of the world. These congregations are worthy of godly admiration. To our shame, even when we had these godly examples right before our very eyes, we made them look like extremists. We told you that *we* were doing the loving thing by not allowing the church to meet together. We made it look as if the true churches were unwise, unloving, and uncharitable. We made it look like those churches that followed God's Word and honored the individual's conscience were fools.[1] We showed you that forcing congregants to wear masks and stay away from each other was the "loving" thing. We're so sorry. We simply didn't have the courage or the backbone to make a stand. Part of us admired those churches that actually lived out the Christian faith, but we just felt much more comfortable in the safe place of conformity to the world. We preferred hearing, "Well done, good and faithful servant" from our governor rather than from the Lord Jesus Christ.

We're sorry we misrepresented Christianity. We made it so painfully easy for you to misunderstand Christianity. We made it shamefully confusing as to

---

[1] "The people who were silenced on lock downs were the people who were *correct* about the lock downs. The people who were censored over masks were the people who were *correct* about the efficacy of masks. The people who challenged the vaccine mandates were *right* about the hazards of those untested vaccines, and they were the people who were not allowed to talk. Many of them had their careers and lives ruined because they tried to talk…So when you say now that you 'did not know,' you need to remember that a bunch of us heard you claiming that you did know. You said that you were following the science when you were only following the television. You legislated as though you knew. You arrested as though you knew. You fined as though you knew. You censored as though you knew" (Doug Wilson, "CT and a Pandemic Amnesty," 7 June 2023, retrieved from www.dougwils.com).

what a true church really is. We made Christianity look like another version of worldliness and humanism. We did this because we based our decisions not on God's Word, but on the shifting sands of the culture around us. We took the powerful, courage-inducing message of Christianity, and, like cowards, we hid it under a bushel. We made physical safety and political correctness more important than the spiritual wellbeing of souls headed for an eternity in either heaven or hell. The gospel teaches that your soul is of far greater value than anything in this life (cf. Mark 8:36). Instead of faithfully proclaiming that message, we shamelessly peddled an insipid and effeminate version of Christianity. America, that is not what Christianity is. What you saw from the vast majority of professing churches was worldliness. We're sorry we didn't have the strength to show you true Christianity.

We're sorry we made Christianity look like a pansy religion that causes her adherents to be unwilling to face the consequences of faithfulness. We had centuries of godly examples of faithfulness to God's Word despite serious consequences and we simply ignored them. We made it seem like our situation – a virus with a low death rate – was worse than anything that had come before. We pretended that our situation was so "unprecedented" that the worthy examples of church history could be admired but not emulated. We pretended the coronavirus was worse than the plague that occurred in Germany when Luther was unwilling to stop meeting with believers.

We acted as if it was worse than the outbreak of the Asiatic cholera in London when Charles Spurgeon kept meeting with Christians. We admit that was just an easy way for us to avoid the cost of discipleship. We have done a really good job of looking to church history for motivation, but we have done a bad job of following in the footsteps of the faithful. We're sorry.

In addition to the examples of church history, we had God's precious Word and the everlasting gospel. True Christianity causes people to be willing to suffer the consequences for faithfulness to Jesus. The true church is composed of those who are willing to suffer loss for the sake of Jesus (Mark 9:34-38) and those who love "not their lives unto the death" (Revelation 12:11). True Christianity involves counting the cost (Luke 14:25-33). It is a message which is so powerful and beautiful and moving that its followers will "count all things loss for the excellence of the knowledge of Christ Jesus my Lord" (Philippians 3:8, NKJV). We pretended like we still believed that. We pretended like we would still lay down our lives for Jesus if we had to, all the while we were unwilling to even meet with fellow believers because we might get sick or fined. Martin Luther once said, "A religion that gives nothing, costs nothing, and suffers nothing, is worth nothing." We presented Christianity as a religion that gives nothing, costs nothing, suffers nothing, and is worth nothing. We're sorry.

Finally, we're sorry that, even years later, we continue to misrepresent what actually happened. Our evangelical leaders continue to write things like,

"Approximately one year ago, North America was hit with the COVID-19 pandemic. Its impact has been so devastating that we'll only know the full extent years from now. We lost the ability to worship corporately for a time."[2] We're sorry we keep perpetuating this lie. We know it's not true. We didn't lose the ability to worship any more than first-century Christians in Rome lost the ability to worship because they could be thrown to the lions or burned alive as human torches. We didn't lose the ability to worship any more than the 16th century Separatists lost the ability to worship because the crown forbade them from gathering outside of the state-sanctioned church.

We're sorry we keep presenting it like this, but it is just so much easier for us to tell ourselves that this was beyond our control, and we were "forced" to no longer follow God's clear command. It's easier for us to keep telling ourselves that we did the right thing, and we had "no choice" but to follow the government's mandate than it is for us to acknowledge that we sinned. Again, we're sorry. We continue to mispresent not only the Christian doctrine of following Jesus and the fellowship of the saints, but also repentance.

We had many good things to *say* to you about Christianity, but we simply chose not to *live* them out. It wasn't forced upon us. We had the ability to continue to meet, but we chose to fall in line with the

---

[2] Donny Friederichsen, "Weariness," 6 March 2021. Retrieved from https://www.ligonier.org/learn/devotionals/weariness-march-2021.

world. We presented Christianity as if it is no different than any other social club. We have no grounds now to critique those "worldly churches" that provided "online services" prior to the coronavirus. We have no grounds now to critique a shallow, take-it-or-leave-it approach to Christian fellowship.

The message we offered during the coronavirus was cheap. It cost us nothing, it asked nothing of you, and it offered nothing to the watching world. It's painful to say it, but the world would have been better off without most professing churches during the past several years. She would have been better served by a small remnant of those faithful churches, accurately representing Christianity, who believed in Jesus and were willing to face the consequences for that belief.

Jesus warned his followers about the scribes and Pharisees. He said this: "The scribes and the Pharisees sit in Moses' seat. Therefore whatever they tell you to observe, that observe and do, but do not do according to their works; for they say, and do not do" (Matthew 23:2-3, NKJV). America, that's us: the leaders of the professing evangelical and Reformed church. By and large, we preached one thing for years. And then, when the rubber met the road, we did something else. Please, take Jesus' advice regarding the scribes and Pharisees and apply it to us. Please don't do what we did. Please don't emulate us. We preached to you, but we didn't practice. We told you of the glorious gospel of Jesus, and the infinite worth of faithfulness to Jesus, no matter the cost, and then we capitulated, without even a fight. We listened to the voice of Fauci instead of the voice of the Chief Shepherd. Our church leaders acted beyond the authority granted them by Christ and told their congregants that they could not gather as a corporate body, and when they could, that they had to wear masks.

America, unless you saw one of those true churches that stood on God's Word (unwilling to cancel fellowship, unwilling to force her congregants to cover their faces and stay away from each other like pagans during a plague) then what you saw this past year was not Christianity. It was worldliness dressed up in Christian garb. True Christianity offers you something different than the world does, but true Christianity will cost you. And there will be consequences. What you saw from most of the professing church was a fearful and cowardly display of the fear of man and the love of this world. If you are willing, please give us another chance. And if we continue to act as we did, without acknowledging how we sinned and admitting our fear, then go find a group of Christians that are willing to face the music for faithfulness. Find a group of Christians who will meet as followers of Jesus, no matter what, without covering their faces in fear. Find a group of Christians who live out their faith. There you will find true Christianity.

CONCLUSION

THE REVELATION

Many Christians have claimed that Covid-19 had a silver lining in that it revealed the true colors of many pastors. This is true, but once churches finally started to reopen many of these same Christians simply returned to pastors who shut down their churches.[1] How has *that revelation* of the church's true colors been helpful? I submit that it has not.

In one sense, I can understand seminary-trained, denominationally-bound, career pastors acting like the world if such behavior doesn't affect the bottom line. They closed the church doors, kept collecting tithes, and then reopened when they were finally willing to spend time with their sheep. Most of the sheep dutifully returned, and everything went back to normal.

However, Christians who are concerned about

---

[1] As I have made clear, a *repentant* pastor, *broken* and *contrite* over scattering the sheep, might be worthy of returning to. A pastor unwilling to humble himself and admit his error, however, is unworthy of a flock. Another question arises: Should Christians wait years and years for this repentance to come? I think three years is long enough.

the failure of pastors during Covid-19 must not perpetuate the problem by enabling cowardly pastors and remaining in churches led by said pastors. Unless the church experiences widespread *repentance*, including repentance over closing the church, she will not be prepared for the next threat. *Now* is the time for pastors to be called to account, be honest about their failings, and openly apologize for scattering the sheep. If those men who scattered the sheep are unwilling to do so, it is time for Christians under their supposed "care" to find another church.

A tying together of two threads is required here. The first thread has to do with the Grace Church narrative of "large numbers" of worshippers showing up when the church was officially closed. The second thread is related to the importance of parishioners calling to account the pastors who scattered them.

As I was speaking once with a pastor who scattered the sheep, I was struck by his reference to the fact that only two people (out of over a thousand) left the church following his decision to cancel church. As mentioned previously, he appealed to this statistic as (in some form) a justification (or validation) of his decision to suspend the assembly and how that decision had not harmed the sheep. I addressed this partially in Chapter 1 but need to address another angle now. This pastor refused to admit he did anything wrong in shutting down the church, and affirmed he will do the same again *if he is convinced* that the same level of risk exists again. And, frankly, why wouldn't he? The fact that over 99% of his parishioners returned after he scattered them is proof positive to him that he can do the same again. A few parishioners who strongly disagree, and yet keep filling the pews (and the offering plate), are no matter.

But there is more to this problem. If a group of one hundred Christians from Pastor John MacArthur's flock, or Pastor Joel Beeke's flock, or Pastor Chris Walker's flock, showed up on the first week that services were cancelled, would those pastors have refused to gather with them? If yes, then it would confirm, in stark terms, their dereliction of duty already evident in their public statements. If not, then it would reveal their cowardice and hypocrisy in saying one thing publicly but then privately bending to the will of the group. I once asked my wife how one of these pastors who scattered the sheep would have reacted if dozens of church members came to him one week after the church closed (perhaps in an outdoor park while their pastor was masked up and going for a government-approved, socially-distanced walk). Imagine, I said, that they came to him distraught and downcast, and pled with him to gather with them, pray with them, sing a Psalm, and share a message of hope from the Bible during this challenging time. I told my wife, "Based on his arguments, he would say something to the effect of, 'No, I will not gather with you. Please go away.'" Maybe he would even run away from them – *members of his own flock*. My wife remonstrated. "He would not do that," she said. "It would look very bad for his reputation if he literally turned them away in a case like that." Of course, she had a point. Making a public announcement of cancelling church, fully in step with the world and largely accepted by the parishioners, is a "safe" decision. The pastor preserves his reputation with the *church* and the *world* (and as it concerns blithe conformity, hardly a difference existed betwixt the two in 2020). At most, a small handful of Christians might be bothered by the suspension of the assembly, but overall, the people will fall in line like everyone else, keep sending their tithe money in, and dutifully return whenever their nanny-pastor tells them it is safe. If, however, the people demanded of their pastor to play the man, things would have been very interesting.

This is where the narrative of Grace Church comes into play. The story is that "large numbers" of people returned and made their way into the worship center to assemble on the Lord's Day months before the church "reopened." If this is true, it does not bode well for MacArthur's reputation – and a good name is to be chosen rather than great riches. If this is true, then MacArthur continued, for months, to declare a message to the world *and* the rest of the church that the assembly was still suspended, while *simultaneously* welcoming those saints that wanted to gather with him and each other on the Lord's Day. Of course, if this happened, it would have had strategic benefits. MacArthur could maintain the allegiance (and money, as he publicly stated was "critical") of those who wanted to gather with him, while also maintaining a public position of submission to the government mandates. Most parishioners likely followed MacArthur's unbiblical cancellation of the assembly, even if *some* came back in clear contradiction of his public statements as their pastor. If MacArthur had acted faithfully from the beginning, and never cancelled church, he *might* have lost most of his parishioners.[2] But, later on, if he turned away the "large numbers" of people returning despite his public statements, then he might have lost *that* group. If the story is accurate, it was a masterfully pragmatic response, from a humanistic, worldly perspective. But it was wrong. MacArthur and his elders would have been better suited to be faithful to God, come what may. The account of a large number of worshippers, in defiance to their pastor's public statements, effectively forcing their pastor to gather with them is demonstrative. These pastors should be ashamed of it, but it is true: For some of these timid and fearful pastors, the faithfulness of their flock is what is needed to keep them in line.

But, alas, as happened in hundreds of churches that shut down, the parishioners confirmed their pastor's nanny-like authority, and then later returned to the church. Unless large numbers of parishioners call these shepherds to account (and are willing to form new churches if these pastors refuse to repent) then we can expect another scattering.

---

[2] More likely, if he had been faithful, he would have been a bold example, inspiring his flock to faithfulness. But, alas, he did not do that, and we will never know how things would have been different had Grace Church stood firm.

For that reason, this book was not primarily written for the compromised pastors. Perhaps appealing to such men is useless at this point – after all, Jesus did say of the blind guides that we ought to "let them alone" (Matthew 15:14) – though I pray they might read it, repent, and find healing. Perhaps this book is primarily for the Christians who found themselves scattered by the seminary-trained shepherds. What should these faithful Christians do now?

A NEW REFORMATION

Hundreds of Christians, disillusioned with the institutional, seminary-trained pastor-class in America, *did* leave churches led by weak men. Throughout the nation, hundreds of Christians realized that their pastors were hirelings. For many of them, they had no place to turn. Some are still scattered, some have (perhaps reluctantly) returned to sit under the teaching of a man who scattered his own people. One thing is clear: The scattering of the sheep in 2020 has revealed the need for a new group of pastors and churches, committed not merely to biblical doctrine but biblical *practice*.

In 16th century England, many pastors (Roman Catholic *and* Protestant) were hirelings, unwilling to do their duty. They were theologically and biblically illiterate and failed to be godly examples to the flock. As the Reformation gained momentum, however, these parish pastors were no longer blindly followed. Christian men and women in England saw through their spiritual façade and demanded something more. The spiritual forebears of the Pilgrims, known as the Separatists, started new churches, outside the authority and blessing of the institutional church of their day. The same thing needs to happen today.

The path forward for American Christians is not in the institutional, seminary-fed, denominationally controlled churches. The denominations, the conventions, the presbyteries, and the seminaries have failed to deal with the pastors who scattered the sheep. *In fact, they have aided and abetted them.* As in 16th century England, the system is corrupt and highly resistant to calls to repentance. The institutional church in America has become a temple of idols – the idols of pastoral prestige, comfort, worldliness, and statism. It is time for Christians to come out from these spiritual whorehouses and preserve the witness of bold Christianity for the next generation. The true church of Jesus Christ needs to heed these words:

> Be not unequally yoked with the infidels: for what fellowship hath righteousness with unrighteousness? and what communion hath light with darkness? And what concord hath Christ with Belial? or what part hath the believer with the infidel? And what agreement hath the Temple of God with idols? for ye are the Temple of the living God: as God hath said, I will dwell among them, and walk there: and I will be their God, and they shall be my people. Wherefore come out from among them, and separate yourselves, saith the Lord, and touch none unclean thing, and I will receive you. And I will be a

Father unto you, and ye shall be my sons and daughters, saith the Lord Almighty.[3]

It is time for Christians to "come out from among" the churches led by false shepherds, unwilling to repent and boldly lead God's people. It might be painful and difficult, but it must be done. The future witness of the true church is worth more than our personal comfort and preferences.

LOVE OF TRADITION

There is a serious obstacle to such a needed reformation. This obstacle also faced the Reformers. It is a love of tradition. The Roman Catholic church (and even the Church of England) had the prestige, the pomp, the tradition, and the authority. For a faithful Christian to leave all that and meet with an unauthorized group of spiritual outcasts in William Brewster's home in Scrooby (the spiritual birthplace of the Pilgrims) was not easy. So it is today.

The big Presbyterian church that shut down for months still has the multiple services and the amazing church choir. It still has the vaulted ceilings and the robed ministers. It still has the stained glass and the aura of holiness. It still has the Reformed conferences and the pastoral staff of doctorate-wielding intellectuals. It still has the coveted *Westminster Confession of Faith* and the illusion of faithfulness in a pagan land.

This love of tradition can also be found in Baptist

---

[3] 2 Corinthians 6:14-18.

churches. People become emotionally attached to groups, conventions, personalities, or celebrity pastors. They become committed to the way things have always been done, rather than being committed to faithfulness and boldness. It is hard for people to leave all these things but leave them they must if one thing is missing: *faithfulness to Christ and his mission in this world.*

We might never see a clearer revelation of the compromise and cowardice of pseudo-shepherds in America than we did in 2020. If *now* is not the time to come out and be separate from such men, the American church might never see reform and revival.

The early Christians – and Christians throughout history, especially in Communist lands – valued bold, genuine Christianity more than vaulted ceilings and architectural beauty. Even today, Christians in China could easily have the nice church building if they simply become a "state church" and submit to the government's religious restrictions. The faithful Christians, however, refuse to compromise. There is nothing inherently wrong with traditions or beautiful church buildings. The problem is when these things prevent Christians from meeting with bold and faithful believers, because their ragtag assembly does not have the "high church" feeling or the rich history of the institutional church.

Given the widespread cowardice and worldliness revealed in the scattering of the sheep, we should not expect the faithful Christians to have the institutional or denominational backing to fund such largesse.

Instead, these Christians will have to be content with Christ, modest meeting places (gyms, basements, etc.), and godly shepherds who refuse to scatter the sheep.

THOSE WHO CAUSE DIVISIONS

Some pastors played a dirty trick when they implied that Christians would cause divisions if they spoke out publicly against the cowardice of the pastors. The following passage was often referenced:

> I appeal to you, brothers, to watch out for those who cause divisions and create obstacles contrary to the doctrine that you have been taught; avoid them. For such persons do not serve our Lord Christ, but their own appetites, and by smooth talk and flattery they deceive the hearts of the naive.[4]

But who *caused* the division in the church? The Christians who spoke up, or the pastors who prevented Christians from gathering with their shepherds? The reality is that the pastors scattering the sheep *caused* the division; the Christians who spoke up were simply pointing it out – they were heeding Paul's exhortation to "watch out" for those who cause division.

And who created the obstacles contrary to sound doctrine? The Christians who spoke up, or the pastors who capped attendance, cancelled service, and required masks? Once again, the pastors

---

[4] Romans 16:17-18, ESV.

scattering the sheep *created* the obstacles; the Christians who spoke up were simply warning others to avoid such men.

Paul's exhortation is to avoid men who cause divisions and create obstacles contrary to sound doctrine. We do well to heed the apostle, and come out from such churches, led by men who "do not serve our Lord Christ." We do well to form new churches, led by men who will not scatter the sheep.

A HEINOUS SIN

The *Westminster Larger Catechism* asks this question: "Are all transgressions of the law of God equally heinous in themselves, and in the sight of God?" The answer: "All transgressions of the law are not equally heinous; but some sins in themselves, and by reason of several aggravations, are more heinous in the sight of God than others." The first of several aggravations listed relates to sins being committed by leaders.

> Sins receive their aggravations...from the persons offending; if they be of riper age, greater experience or grace, eminent for profession, gifts, place, office, guides to others, and whose example is likely to be followed by others.

The sin of scattering the sheep was more heinous than the sins of Anthony Fauci or state governors, because the pastors scattering the sheep were "eminent for profession" and spiritual "guides to others," and their example is likely to be followed by others.[5]

May God have mercy and grant repentance to the shepherds who scattered the sheep. Otherwise, may God guide the sheep to find faithful and courageous pastors.

---

[5] "For leaders not to lead is an affront against nature itself, as when clouds are all puff and no rain, or trees are all leaf and no fruit. Such leaders are 'shepherds who feed only themselves' (Jude 1:12). They run when they see a wolf coming (John 10:12). Or they are the wolf. 'Woe to the shepherds…Should not the shepherds feed the flocks?' (Ezekiel 34:2)" (Andrée Seu Peterson, *World*, Volume 38, Number 18, p. 70).

APPENDIX A

PASTOR JOE JEWART'S STATEMENT CONCERNING CHURCH CLOSURES

Joe Jewart is pastor of Calvary Baptist Church in Natrona Heights, Pennsylvania. The following statement was released by Jewart in 2023.

•••

I believe Covid-19 has been a valuable lesson for the Church. It has made us think about the spheres of authority and the boundaries God has established for them in this world. When the governing authorities mandated that all non-essential businesses be shut down due to Covid-19, they included the church as being in the non-essential category, and many American evangelical churches willingly submitted to it. The pastors of these churches were, and still are, theologically unprepared to thoughtfully consider the implications of their submission to such mandates.

I officially became a part-time pastor in March of 2019 and, in 2020, I willingly submitted to the shutdown until May 24, 2020. I realize that it was truly foolish and unbiblical for me to allow the state to deem God's church as non-essential, especially since the state continued to view the murder of babies (abortion) as an essential component of American life.

So, when we opened on May 24, I preached on Revelation 1:4-8 concerning the Kingship of Christ. Covid-19, in the clearest way, revealed to all of us the god of our culture. America decided that it was essential for us to continue the ultimate expression of self-worship, which is sacrificing children, and to discontinue the public worship of Christ – the one who was sacrificed for the salvation of the world. This was much more than just a political issue. This was an issue concerning worship, which obviously has political implications. Cultus (worship) is the foundation of culture and is inescapably expressed outwardly in culture. Worship never limits itself to the hearts of individuals. Worship comes out of the hearts of individuals who make up communities, nations, and cultures. Our cultural and political views on civil, family, and church matters are fundamentally built upon who or what we worship. Another way of putting this is that we build our cultural and political views based on who we think is the ultimate King, or Sovereign.

When churches bowed to the decree of the shutdown, not only did they shut down America's fundamental and essential need to worship the Triune God, but they were also preaching to the whole world a false gospel that Christ is not the king. Pastors who preached this false gospel by acting in accordance with the shutdowns need to humble themselves and repent or leave their pastoral position. I say that with humility, love, and concern for the body of Christ. I'm speaking as a pastor who sinfully complied with the humanistic government. I had the responsibility to lead the church to the throne of Christ, but instead I led them to bow before the state. Thank God for the grace found in Jesus Christ. In Him all sins are washed clean and forgotten. So, pastor, if you have taught your people to bow before the state instead of Christ by shutting down the local church that God has placed in your care, I plead with you to repent.

The word church in the Greek should be familiar to us. It is the word Ekklesia. It basically means congregation, or assembly. Literally, it means a group of people called out. The LXX version of the Old Testament makes use of this term for the people of Israel (Deut. 31:30; Josh. 8:35; 1 Chron. 29:1). God called Israel out of Egypt to redeem them, to form them into a holy nation, for the purpose of His glory. Stephen, in Acts 7:38, uses this Greek word to describe Israel. The ESV translates it as "congregation." There is an interesting aspect of this word which I think is lost in the church today. The normal use of Ekklesia not only refers to private religious gatherings, but to public gatherings, or political assemblies. As the Thayer's dictionary puts it, "A gathering of citizens called out from their homes into some public place." If you read the Scriptures closely, you will understand that public assemblies are inherently religious and political. The Church is not only a temple/building, it is not only a family, but it is a people of a New Kingdom with a real King. As soon as you make the claim, "Jesus is king," you are making a public and political declaration. The Church is not a private religious gathering without public influence. We are citizens of New Jerusalem. This means that the church influences the fallen kingdoms of men to join the unshakable kingdom of God under the Kingship of Jesus Christ. When our public assemblies closed down, we were no longer operating as the Ekklesia. We stopped being a public assembly. We rejected our duty to bring the crown rights of Christ into the public place. The Church should never again bow to the humanistic claim that the public worship of the true and living God is non-essential.

APPENDIX B

MESSAGES FROM THE SHEEP

The following segments were taken from messages that were sent to the author. They are demonstrative of the experience of thousands of Christians who were scattered by the shepherds.

•••

S.M. and M.M. (England), written in June 2021: Today your message "Covid Apology to America" ended up being forwarded onto our Christians Against Lockdown Telegram Messenger App. I just wanted to say a big thank you! Here in the UK, although most churches have now opened (under tight restrictions) by far the vast majority closed their doors for the majority of last year. Frustratingly, my husband and I initially were lone voices in our firm belief this was wrong, but slowly a small minority of Christians' eyes have been opened.

A.D. (Netherlands), written in August 2021: I feel less alone having read your book. Something just slotted into place. All the things you mention in your book are true for the church I attend…Covid has ravaged the church I attend, with lockdowns and all the other rules. It no longer feels like a friendly, welcoming, and social church anymore. It becomes easier and easier to only half listen to the sermons coming from the pulpit. I feel isolated from the community…maybe because there is little real community. The congregation seems scared, and too willing to keep their distance. The elders have become more like police officers, enforcing social distancing, etc. Nobody really laughs any more, and everyone has become seemingly stiffer, not knowing what to do next. Spontaneity has been lost. As no coffee is served at the end of services now, people go home soon and there is less contact. People have fallen away from the church, some to attend elsewhere, others simply stay at home. Still others are neither totally in nor totally out, but like myself still make regular financial contributions, without attending as often. The financial situation is dire, and the congregation has been asked to contribute 30% more. We used to be one of the most welcoming churches around….no longer though!

J.D. (Australia), written in August 2021: I'm a Christian psychologist [in]…Australia. We're in the midst of a dark time [concerning] COVID as our lockdowns get more severe and random, yet our COVID cases keep increasing in line with our vaccination rates. You may have heard we have the military on the streets of Sydney keeping people in lockdown and forcing people to be vaccinated. We have digressed to tyranny so quickly, and I have been shocked and appalled at the church's (and general population's) apathy to such ludicrous overreach and nonsensical responses. And I have felt like I was on another planet, or must have gone crazy, as my beliefs and attitudes are the opposite of everyone else's it seems.

Tonight, I have been comforted to have met with two Christian ladies from my church for the first time, whom I had discovered share my views. One has not been coming to church for 16 months as she is not allowed in the door without a mask and QR code, which she is convicted she should stand against.

I also work in a Christian school as their School Psychologist. I have been struck by the degree of fear and panic amongst the staff around this, which I find oppressive. They are not only succumbing to the fear of the world around the COVID lies but are exceeding the world's fears and enforcing even greater restrictions. I have been called to the Principal's Office and chastised for the one social media post I have made which was an invitation to one of the first freedom rallies.

After going to Sydney (in lockdown) last week for emergency dental work, which was approved and discussed with my Principal, I returned to work as planned and had staff members in such a panic that they went home in the middle of the day, so uncomfortable were they with my presence. I was asked to get a COVID test (not required by the "regime") and to stay home until I had a negative result…Coming across your piece "COVID Apology to the World on Behalf of the Evangelical Church" was a Godsend tonight…The situation is serious…I cannot fathom the degree of fear that flies in the face of our professed faith. And the idolatry of the Vaccine which is touted from the pulpit as being our savior (they fall short of using that word).

M.C. (United States), written in October 2023: Thank you for your book, *Essential Service*. I think that was the very first resource on this issue that I found. It helped me greatly. Unfortunately, my church was closed for a full year. Then they reopened, but banned non-masking people for one week short of a second year. I was effectively alone for two years. I have never fully recovered. I am in a different church now. But it's been hard. I lost all my friends.

APPENDIX C

SIX REASONS EVERY PASTOR SHOULD REQUIRE MASKS AND SOCIAL DISTANCING AT CHURCH (SATIRE)

The following was written by Chris Hume and originally published as a blog post at ReformedHope.com on February 16, 2021. It is a satirical piece. Satire entails the use of humor, irony, exaggeration, or ridicule to expose and criticize vice.

• • •

I've said it before, navigating pastoral ministry is tricky business. But one thing that you can take to the bank is that requiring masks and social distancing at church is an outstanding pastoral decision. The nice thing is that you don't really have to think about it. The government and health experts have already done all the thinking for you – your job is to do what they say. But just in case you are still unsure if you should require churchgoers to wear masks and social distance, here are six reasons why every pastor should require these wise and loving measures.

1. You Will Be Fitting in (and Helping Others Fit in Too)

One of your most important duties as a pastor is to fit in with other pastors. If a majority of other churches have chosen to enforce mask mandates, they are obviously correct. Throughout history, it has always been the case that the majority is correct. Christians, and especially Christian leaders, are never called to stand alone in the world. John Knox was definitely wrong when he said, "A man with God is always in the majority." Furthermore, your duty is to help church members fit in with the world around them. It's not helpful for Christians to look different than the world. You want visitors to walk into your church and say, "Hey, everyone here behaves just like the rest of the world – this seems like a good place for me!" You want outsiders to understand that the church reacts to the virus just like the unbelieving world. This is how we reach the lost. As you lovingly lead your people by requiring them to wear masks, you will be helping others conform to the world, which is better than being transformed.

2. You Will Encourage Everyone to Trust the Government

Christians should be innocent as serpents and wise as doves. This is especially true when it comes to government mandates relating to the church. Because the government is worthy of our complete trust and obedience, there is no need to question any of their decisions. Anything they tell us to do is undoubtedly for our good and should be adhered to rigorously, especially as it relates to church matters. By requiring face masks and social distancing when your church gathers, you will be helping your congregants to realize that every mandate from Washington, D.C. is worthy of our unquestioning obedience. Despite our government's immaculate track record of always caring for life, from the preborn to the elderly, some naïve church members still stubbornly think that the government is not qualified to give such directives. These foolish Christians overreact to the fact that the government allows a few abortions each year. Overall, our government is manifestly spotless when it comes to protecting life. Any mandate to wear a mask or stay away from other Christians during church should be submitted to so that more people will trust that our government always knows what is best. It should go without saying, but I'll say it just to be safe (and safety is always first in Christianity): the government obviously has the best interests of the church of Jesus Christ in mind whenever it makes any decision. In earlier times, before Christians knew better, the church stood independent of government regulations and mandates. Some asinine Christians (like the Pilgrims) were even willing to face imprisonment and torture to be free of government intrusion in matters of church life. Thankfully, pastors today don't have to be like them. It is now not only acceptable to let the government tell the church what to do, but also the most loving thing.

3. By Binding the Consciences of All Believers, You Will Weed Out Dangerous, Independent Thinkers from Your Church

By using your authority as a pastor to require all church members to wear masks, you will do the good work of separating the wheat from the chaff. Why would you want to have supposed "Christians" in your church who think that individual believers should be able to make up their own minds about wearing a mask or social distancing? Those types of people certainly cause divisions and create obstacles. They are probably also conspiracy theorists. If you do not require masks, you will not only allow these dangerous parishioners to think for themselves, but you will be implicitly allowing them to encourage others to think for themselves as well. This is the last thing you want to do as a pastor. Your job is to do all the thinking for your church. Since you went to seminary, you are clearly the most qualified to decide if everyone should wear a mask. Your sheep are not able to make these decisions for themselves. By lovingly forcing everyone to wear a mask, you will likely get rid of those wolves who foolishly think you do not have the authority to bind the consciences of believers regarding the Lord's Day assembly. Stand firm in your conviction that everyone should have the exact same convictions about masks; lord it over the people if you must. Your church, and world for that matter, will be a much better place without these people who think they can make decisions for themselves; self-government is so passé.

4. You Will Be Showing Your Support for the Government Mandated Shutdown of Your Congregants' Businesses

Social distancing requirements have led many family businesses to close their doors indefinitely. There is no question that this was the right decision. It is far more important that we slow the inevitable spread of the coronavirus than that people can support themselves and their families. If even one person dies because of the coronavirus, we have failed as a nation. But if someone loses his business, cannot support his family, and turns to drugs, alcohol, and suicide, our hands are clean. This is the price we pay for safety. We will stoically accept such consequences — it's the loving thing to do. In the extremely rare event that people in your church lose a business because of the government mandates, your job as a church leader is to show your faithfulness to the government's decisions so these people will feel better about being out of work. By enforcing mask and social distancing requirements, your church will be an example to the community around you, a city on a hill. Your church can lead the way in helping businessowners submit to all the government mandates, even if it means Christians lose their jobs and have to rely on government money. This is the sacrifice you have been called to as a minister of the gospel. If you don't follow this advice, the results could be disastrous. If you don't comply with mask regulations, you might unwittingly encourage businessowners in your congregation to do the same thing. Obviously, if a business does not religiously enforce mask mandates and social distancing, all employees and customers will get the virus, and probably die. Businessowner Alfie Oakes committed the unpardonable sin of allowing customers to choose whether to wear a mask. He is a boar in the Lord's vineyard. Avoid such heretics like the plague (or the coronavirus…same thing, right?) and do not let them in your church (unless they repent and don a mask).

5. You Will Help Christians Understand True Science

In the past, before scientific advances helped the church realize many of her errors, Christians used to believe that God created humans with immune systems. There are still some fundamentalists who believe this today. Now that we know better, it would be unconscionable to proport the lie that our bodies are able to develop immunity to viruses and diseases. To be honest, it is disgusting that some parents continue to teach their children this fairy tale. By ensuring that everyone covers their face and stays six feet away from one another, you will reinforce the undisputed truth that our bodies were not designed to interact with microbes and develop natural immunity. Churches should definitely not be the place for people to interact with other people. If you enforce these measures, concerned mothers can rest assured that their children will be much better prepared to face the world around them, having been sheltered not only from the coronavirus, but also a bunch of other deadly microbes. You'll be a hero.

6. *You Will Ensure Unity by Making Everyone Act the Same Way*

It doesn't make sense to recommend that only people truly concerned about contracting the virus wear a mask, or face shield, or hazmat suit, if everyone else isn't also required to wear a mask. If some people are worried about getting the virus, then it makes perfect sense to make everyone else wear a mask too. Anytime anyone is concerned about something, then everyone else should also act as if they are concerned about it too. This is what it means to love others. Love means we accept whatever someone else believes. If everyone isn't required to wear masks, then the people that are really concerned about getting infected would be forced to make their own decisions about how to avoid the virus. They might even have to think about how concerned about the virus they really are. In any case, you don't want to be the cause of those things. You want everyone in your herd, or flock, to wear a mask until further notice. In this way, no one will get the virus and the group will develop herd immunity. And, if you are ever tempted to question the wisdom of these mandates, just remember that "we are all in this together." As long as everyone is acting in "unity," nothing else really matters.

ALSO BY CHRIS HUME

Essential Service: Coronavirus and the Assembly of the Saints (2020)

Vote Christian: Biblical Principles for Voting (2021)

Seven Statist Sins: The Capital Vices of Civil Government in American Society (2023)

The Good News of the Covenant: Thinking Covenantally About the Gospel of Jesus Christ (forthcoming, 2024)

THE
LANCASTER PATRIOT

The Lancaster Patriot is leading a movement to restore truthful and ethical media in Lancaster County, Pennsylvania. Our goal is to provide a distinctly Christian voice in the realm of media, commentary, and literature. From podcasts to editorials to news stories to books, we are seeking to bring all things under the crown rights of King Jesus. We also provide a venue for the clash of ideas and worldviews, hosting debates on politics, law, and education, and regularly inviting detractors to publicly engage.

In our journalism, we are committed to being truthful, ethical, and investigative – providing coverage without fear or favor, locally focused first, and always committed to Christian principles and core traditional values. In our commentary, we are committed to standing on the Law-Word of God as the source of justice.

thelancasterpatriot.com | patreon.com/thelancasterpatriot

Made in the USA
Middletown, DE
21 December 2023

46631333R00104